T0322899

M. Sandra Wood
Editor

Bioterrorism and Political Violence: Web Resources

Bioterrorism and Political Violence: Web Resources has been co-published simultaneously as *Internet Reference Services Quarterly*, Volume 6, Numbers 3/4 2002.

Pre-publication
REVIEWS,
COMMENTARIES,
EVALUATIONS . . .

"This volume is much more than the listing of 'Web Resources' promised in the subtitle–it is A VALUABLE TOOL for librarians and others seeking up-to-date information on terrorism and violence. In addition to an impressive listing of authoritative Web resources, most of which can be expected to both endure and be kept current, the authors include background material and unexpected definitions of Bioterrorism. The scope of this endeavor is broad and inclusive, with an unexpected chapter on Islamic terrorist groups and a very helpful chapter on disaster preparedness for hospitals and medical librarians."

Robert S. Lyle, MLS
Library Director
VA Medical Center, Philadelphia

More pre-publication
REVIEWS, COMMENTARIES, EVALUATIONS . . .

" **A** TIMELY AND MOST WEL-COME RESOURCE. . . . The contributors provide clear background information and definitions, along with quality-filtered reviews by health sciences librarians of relevant and reliable Web sites geared to both professionals and consumers. A very useful feature of many of the sections is the special mention of Web sites that contain FAQs on subjects such as preparedness, coping, food safety, and of course, anthrax."

Patricia Tomasulo, MLS, AHIP
*Coordinator of Information Resources
and User Services
Ehrman Medical Library
New York University School
of Medicine*

The Haworth Information Press
An Imprint of The Haworth Press, Inc.

Bioterrorism
and Political Violence:
Web Resources

Bioterrorism and Political Violence: Web Resources has been co-published simultaneously as *Internet Reference Services Quarterly*, Volume 6, Numbers 3/4 2002.

Internet Reference Services Quarterly Monographic "Separates"

Below is a list of "separates," which in serials librarianship means a special issue simultaneously published as a special journal issue or double-issue and as a "separate" hardbound monograph. (This is a format which we also call a "DocuSerial.")

"Separates" are published because specialized libraries or professionals may wish to purchase a specific thematic issue by itself in a format which can be separately cataloged and shelved, as opposed to purchasing the journal on an on-going basis. Faculty members may also more easily consider a "separate" for classroom adoption.

"Separates" are carefully classified separately with the major book jobbers so that the journal tie-in can be noted on new book order slips to avoid duplicate purchasing.

You may wish to visit Haworth's website at . . .

http://www.HaworthPress.com

. . . to search our online catalog for complete tables of contents of these separates and related publications.

You may also call 1-800-HAWORTH (outside US/Canada: 607-722-5857), or Fax: 1-800-895-0582 (outside US/Canada: 607-771-0012), or e-mail at:

getinfo@haworthpressinc.com

Bioterrorism and Political Violence: Web Resources, edited by M. Sandra Wood, MLS, MBA (Vol. 6, No. 3/4, 2002). _Describes how to find reliable information on bioterrorism via the Internet._

The Challenge of Internet Literacy: The Instruction-Web Convergence, edited by Lyn Elizabeth M. Martin, BA, MLS (Vol. 2, No. 2/3, 1997). _"A source of valuable advice. . . . Recommended for institutions that collect library science materials on a comprehensive level." (Library & Information Science Annual 1999)_

Bioterrorism and Political Violence: Web Resources

M. Sandra Wood
Editor

Bioterrorism and Political Violence: Web Resources has been co-published simultaneously as *Internet Reference Services Quarterly*, Volume 6, Numbers 3/4 2002.

The Haworth Information Press
An Imprint of
The Haworth Press, Inc.
New York • London • Oxford

Published by

The Haworth Information Press®, 10 Alice Street, Binghamton, NY 13904-1580 USA

The Haworth Information Press® is an imprint of The Haworth Press, Inc., 10 Alice Street, Binghamton, NY 13904-1580 USA.

Bioterrorism and Political Violence: Web Resources has been co-published simultaneously as *Internet Reference Services Quarterly*, Volume 6, Numbers 3/4 2002.

Cover design by Jennifer Gaska.

Library of Congress Cataloging-in-Publication Data

Bioterrorism and political violence : web resources / M. Sandra Wood, editor.
     p. cm.
     "Co-published simultaneously as Internet reference services quarterly, volume 6, numbers 3/4 2002."
     Includes bibliographical references and index.
     ISBN 0-7890-1964-7 (alk. paper)–ISBN 0-7890-1965-5 (alk. paper)
     1. Bioterrorism–Computer network resources. 2. Terrorism–Computer network resources. 3. Political violence–Computer network resources. 4. Web sites–Directories. I. Wood, M. Sandra. II. Internet reference services quarterly.
HV6431.B562 2002
025.06′303625–dc21
                                                                                              2002006071

Indexing, Abstracting & Website/Internet Coverage

This section provides you with a list of major indexing & abstracting services. That is to say, each service began covering this periodical during the year noted in the right column. Most Websites which are listed below have indicated that they will either post, disseminate, compile, archive, cite or alert their own Website users with research-based content from this work. (This list is as current as the copyright date of this publication.)

Abstracting, Website/Indexing Coverage . . . . Year When Coverage Began

- *Applied Social Sciences Index & Abstracts (ASSIA)*
  (Online: ASSI via Data-Star) (CDRom: ASSIA Plus)
  <www.csa.com> 1996

- *BUBL Information Service: An Internet-based Information*
  Service for the UK higher education community
  <URL:http://bubl.ac.uk/> 1996

- *CINAHL (Cumulative Index to Nursing & Allied Health*
  Literature), in print, EBSCO, and SilverPlatter,
  Data-Star, and PaperChase. (Support materials
  include Subject Heading List, Database Search
  Guide, and instructional video) <www.cinahl.com> 1996

- *CNPIEC Reference Guide: Chinese National Directory*
  of Foreign Periodicals 1996

- *Computer Literature Index* 1997

- *Computing Reviews* 1996

- *Current Awareness Abstracts of Library & Information*
  Management Literature, ASLIB (UK) 2000

- *Current Cites [Digital Libraries] [Electronic Publishing]*
  [Multimedia & Hypermedia] [Networks & Networking]
  [General] 1998

- *Current Index to Journals in Education* 2002

(continued)

(continued)

*Special Bibliographic Notes related to special journal issues
(separates) and indexing/abstracting:*

- indexing/abstracting services in this list will also cover material in any "separate" that is co-published simultaneously with Haworth's special thematic journal issue or DocuSerial. Indexing/abstracting usually covers material at the article/chapter level.
- monographic co-editions are intended for either non-subscribers or libraries which intend to purchase a second copy for their circulating collections.
- monographic co-editions are reported to all jobbers/wholesalers/approval plans. The source journal is listed as the "series" to assist the prevention of duplicate purchasing in the same manner utilized for books-in-series.
- to facilitate user/access services all indexing/abstracting services are encouraged to utilize the co-indexing entry note indicated at the bottom of the first page of each article/chapter/contribution.
- this is intended to assist a library user of any reference tool (whether print, electronic, online, or CD-ROM) to locate the monographic version if the library has purchased this version but not a subscription to the source journal.
- individual articles/chapters in any Haworth publication are also available through the Haworth Document Delivery Service (HDDS).

Bioterrorism and Political Violence: Web Resources

CONTENTS

"HOT" BIBLIOGRAPHIES

ABOUT THE EDITOR

M. Sandra Wood, MLS, MBA, is Librarian, Reference and Database Services, of The Milton S. Hershey Medical Center at The Pennsylvania State University in Hershey. She holds the academic rank of librarian and has over thirty-one years of experience as a medical reference librarian, including the areas of general reference services, management of reference services, database and Internet searching, and user instruction. Ms. Wood has been widely published in the field of medical reference and is Editor of the journals *Medical Reference Services Quarterly* and *Health Care on the Internet* (Haworth) and of several Haworth books, including *Men's Health on the Internet, Women's Health on the Internet, Health Care Resources on the Internet: A Guide for Librarians and Health Care Consumers,* and *Cancer Resources on the Internet.* She is a member of the Medical Library Association and the Special Libraries Association, and has served on the MLA's Board of Directors as Treasurer. Ms. Wood is also a Fellow of the Medical Library Association.

Preface

The events of September 11, 2001 shocked a nation and the world. The terrorist acts of that day, followed by the anthrax scares in the fall of 2001, made the threat of political violence and bioterrorism a reality for the people of the United States. These events, followed by the continuing War on Terrorism, will continue to have a worldwide impact on the people of the U.S. and the world for the immediate and foreseeable future.

As the terrorist acts of 9/11 unfolded, many people turned to the Internet for current information, not only for news as it happened, but for information about the possibilities of what *could* happen with political terrorist and bioterrorist attacks. Government and civil agencies, the health care community, and the general public sought reliable, current information about biological agents and agents of mass destruction, treatments for potential diseases caused by biological agents that could be used by terrorists, information about government agencies in place for disaster prevention, and how to plan for a disaster.

Given the need to disseminate information quickly, it was only natural for the U.S. government, and other agencies and organizations, to turn to the Internet as the best way to make this information available, both to the general public and to the people responsible for disaster planning. Perhaps the most difficult part of accessing information via the Internet is determining the best sites to go to. Overshadowing all of the official government and quality health information sites is an overwhelming amount of "junk" and bad information.

It became evident immediately in the fall of 2001 that Web users would need to be guided to appropriate material on bioterrorism and political violence. In response, many individual sites have sprung up on the Internet as directories to locate quality information about terrorism.

[Haworth co-indexing entry note]: "Preface." Wood, M. Sandra. Co-published simultaneously in *Internet Reference Services Quarterly* (The Haworth Information Press, an imprint of The Haworth Press, Inc.) Vol. 6, No. 3/4, 2002, pp. xv-xvii; and: *Bioterrorism and Political Violence: Web Resources* (ed: M. Sandra Wood) The Haworth Information Press, an imprint of The Haworth Press, Inc., 2002, pp. xiii-xv. Single or multiple copies of this article are available for a fee from The Haworth Document Delivery Service [1-800-HAWORTH, 9:00 a.m. - 5:00 p.m. (EST). E-mail address: getinfo@haworthpressinc.com].

xiii

Many of these sites tend to focus on very specific aspects, e.g., anthrax, or September 11. Often, they simply offer links to other Web sites, with no explanation of what will be found at the site. The need existed for an overview of Web sites covering all aspects of terrorism, from the events of September 11 through disaster planning. This volume is intended to fill that need. While some might question the use of a print volume versus putting up an actual Web site, it should be pointed out that a Web site can be just as static as a print volume. In selecting sites for inclusion in this volume authors have attempted to choose sites with stable locations, such as government sites or well known associations, institutions, or agencies that will continue to be available via the Internet for years to come. When URLs of individual documents are given, users of this volume are reminded that updates of documents do occur, and that they should go back to the main page of the Web site to re-locate a more current version of the document they are seeking.

   Each author was asked to focus on a specific aspect of political violence and bioterrorism, selecting quality, authoritative sites, but it was inevitable that there would be an overlap within these articles of the Web sites that were selected. As had been found by the U.S. government in determining the need for an Office of Homeland Security, there is significant duplication and overlap in the functions and roles of existing government agencies themselves. Web sites that are listed in multiple articles should be viewed as "key" in locating bioterrorism information.

   In the initial article, Hinegardner and Mayo overview bioterrorism Web sites. In "Selected Bioterrorism Web Sites for the Health Care Community and Consumer," they focus on government organizations, educational institutions, and professional associations to provide a core of important Web sites on bioterrorism. In the next article, Holtum and Roth focus on "Anthrax Resources on the Web." Following the fall 2001 anthrax scares, the quest for information about diagnosis, symptoms, treatment, and prevention of this particular disease has been overwhelming. In "Information for Immunity: Internet Resources on Biological Agents as Terrorist Weapons," Forger and Knight focus on Web sites about biological and chemical agents other than anthrax, including bacteria, fungi, viruses, and toxins. Maragliano overviews Internet resources about Islamic terrorist groups in "Political Violence and Islam: Definitions and Web Resources." Because of the recent attacks in the U.S., some sites on national security are included in her article. In "September 11, 2001: Special Web Sites," Bronson Fitzpatrick begins with a personal account about September 11, which she experienced from NYU Health Center, near the World Trade Center. Her article focuses on Web sites specific to September 11, including sites established as a tribute to people who died that day from the attacks on the WTC, the Pentagon, and the plane downed in Pennsylvania. The terrorist attacks generated psychological and emotional reactions, felt by people worldwide. In their article, "Surviving the Attack: Web Resources on the Emotional Impact of Terrorism," Gallagher and Ascher have compiled a selection of reliable Web sites dealing with posttraumatic stress disorder, including how to help children deal with terrorism. The possibility of terrorists acquiring nuclear weapons has become a real concern following September 11. Swartz covers this topic in "Nuclear Terrorism: A Selection of Internet Resources." In "It Wasn't Raining When Noah Built the Ark: Disaster Preparedness for Hospital and Medical Librarians Post September 11," Volesko has geared her extensive article toward the critical role that health professionals play in responding to a disaster. While the article is directed toward hospitals, health care agencies, and health care professionals, any public agency responsible for disaster planning or responding to a disaster/terrorist threat should be aware of the official documents and Web sites listed here. In "News Sites: Locating News as It Happens," Wood provides a highly selected list of sites intended to locate current news information, along with archived information about September 11 and the War on Terrorism, as reported by the news media.

With the plethora of information available on the Internet, it is hoped that this volume will be useful to persons–both professionals and the general public–looking for quality Web sites about September 11, bioterrorism, and political violence and terrorism.

M. Sandra Wood

Selected Bioterrorism Web Sites for the Health Care Community and Consumer

Patricia G. Hinegardner
Alexa Mayo

SUMMARY. For the people of the United States, the threat of bioterrorism has become a reality. To respond to the recent outbreak of anthrax cases and to prepare for future threats, the health care community, civil authorities, and general public need access to reliable, up-to-date information. The Web is one tool that can be used to deliver this information. This article briefly defines bioterrorism, identifies major biological agents, looks at the potential impact of an attack and provides a selected list of Web sites for consumers and health care professionals. The selection criteria used to evaluate the sites included sponsorship, currency, content (factual information), and audience. Most of the sites are from government organizations, educational institutions, or professional associations. *[Article copies available for a fee from The Haworth Document Delivery Service: 1-800-HAWORTH. E-mail address: <getinfo@haworthpressinc.com> Website: <http://www.HaworthPress.com> © 2002 by The Haworth Press, Inc. All rights reserved.]*

KEYWORDS. Bioterrorism, Internet

Patricia G. Hinegardner (phinegar@umaryland.edu) is Coordinator of Specialized Information Services/Web Manager and Alexa Mayo (alexa@umaryland.edu) is Assistant Director of Information and Instructional Services, both at Health Sciences and Human Services Library, University of Maryland, Baltimore, MD 21201.

[Haworth co-indexing entry note]: "Selected Bioterrorism Web Sites for the Health Care Community and Consumer." Hinegardner, Patricia G., and Alexa Mayo. Co-published simultaneously in *Internet Reference Services Quarterly* (The Haworth Information Press, an imprint of The Haworth Press, Inc.) Vol. 6, No. 3/4, 2002, pp. 1-15; and: *Bioterrorism and Political Violence: Web Resources* (ed: M. Sandra Wood) The Haworth Information Press, an imprint of The Haworth Press, Inc., 2002, pp. 1-15. Single or multiple copies of this article are available for a fee from The Haworth Document Delivery Service [1-800-HAWORTH, 9:00 a.m. - 5:00 p.m. (EST). E-mail address: getinfo@haworthpressinc.com].

INTRODUCTION

The events of September 11, 2001 and the subsequent outbreak of anthrax cases have created an unprecedented demand for information about terrorism. Bioterrorism, a form of terrorism, is the use of biological agents, such as infectious microbes or toxins, to produce illness or death in people, animals, or plants. Biological agents can be dispersed as aerosols or airborne particles. They can be used to contaminate food or water.[1]

The Centers for Disease Control and Prevention (CDC) defines three categories of biologic agents with the potential to be used as weapons. The categories are based on four criteria: ease of dissemination or transmission, potential for major public health impact (high mortality), potential for public panic and social disruption, and requirements for public health preparedness. Category A is a list of the agents of highest concern: *Bacillus anthracis* (anthrax), *Yersinia pestis* (plague), variola major (smallpox), *Clostridium botulinum* toxin (botulism), *Francisella tularensis* (tularemia), filoviruses (Ebola hemorrhagic fever, Margurg hemorrhagic fever) and arenaviruses Lassa (Lassa fever), Junin (Argentine hemorrhagic fever) and related viruses.[2]

The first cases of bioterrorism-related anthrax exposure occurred on the heels of the September 11th terrorist attacks. As of November 14, 2001, a total of 22 cases of anthrax had been identified; 10 were confirmed inhalation anthrax and 12 (seven confirmed and five suspected) were cutaneous anthrax.[3] Approximately 300 postal and other facilities have been tested for B. anthracis spores and about 32,000 persons have initiated antimicrobial prophylaxis following potential exposure to B. anthracis at workplaces in Florida, District of Columbia, New Jersey, and New York City.[4] In addition to persons exposed to a biological agent, it is estimated that from 10 to 20 "worried well" per each truly ill victim also seek medical treatment.[5] The impact on the health care system of treating those who become ill, those who have been exposed, and the "worried well" who need reassurance could become overwhelming.

The rapid dissemination of reliable, up-to-date information among public health officials, front-line health care providers, and law enforcement authorities is a key factor in responding to the threat of bioterrorism.[6] It is also important to enhance awareness and training of front-line health care providers and to provide comprehensive information for the public. The Web is one tool that can be used to deliver this information.

The following is a list of selected Web sites for consumers and health care professionals. The selection criteria used to evaluate these sites included sponsorship, currency, content (factual information), and audience. Most of the sites are from government organizations, educational institutions, or professional associations. Images of several sites are included.

CONSUMER RESOURCES

MEDLINEplus (National Library of Medicine) <http://medlineplus.gov>

This is a consumer-oriented Web site (see Figure 1) established by the National Library of Medicine, the world's largest biomedical library. MEDLINEplus provides several Web pages devoted to issues of bioterrorism including:

Disasters and Emergency Preparedness
<http://www.nlm.nih.gov/medlineplus/
    disastersandemergencypreparedness.html>

Biological and Chemical Weapons
<http://www.nlm.nih.gov/medlineplus/
    biologicalandchemicalweapons.html>

Anthrax
<http://www.nlm.nih.gov/medlineplus/anthrax.html>

Smallpox
<http://www.nlm.nih.gov/medlineplus/smallpox.html>

Each page contains links to authoritative information on that subject, as well as an optional link to a pre-formulated MEDLINE search that provides journal article citations on the subject. Some topics, including anthrax, offer interactive tutorials that use animated graphics to explain procedures or conditions in easy-to-read language. Selected information is in Spanish. Additional MEDLINEplus resources are available in directories, dictionaries, and drug information sources.

FIGURE 1. MEDLINEplus

Center for Mental Health Services
Knowledge Exchange Network (KEN)
Disaster Mental Health
<http://www.mentalhealth.org/>

The purpose of this federally sponsored organization is to help states "improve and increase the quality and range of their treatment, rehabilitation, and support services for people with mental illness, their families, and communities." The Knowledge Exchange Network provides consumers with a wealth of mental health information. The "Disaster Mental Health" section includes "Tips for Talking About Disasters," which links to resources related to children and adolescents, adults, and emergency and disaster response workers. Selected information is in Spanish. There is also a "Bioterrorism Resources" section.

healthfinder®–Anthrax and Other Bioterrorism Information
<http://www.healthfinder.gov/anthrax_bioterrorism.htm>

Developed by the U.S. Department of Health and Human Services in collaboration with other federal agencies, healthfinder® is a gateway to consumer health information. It was created "to improve consumer access to selected health information from government agencies, their many partner organizations, and other reliable sources that serve the public interest." The "Anthrax and Other Bioterrorism" page provides links to information resources organized under five major headings. "Updates" provides links to information from the CDC, the U.S. Postal Service, and to recent statements from the Surgeon General. "FAQs/Fact" contains information on various biological agents (anthrax, smallpox, botulism and pneumonic plague). "Treatment" provides information on Doxycycline and Cipro. "Key Links" lists government and organization Web sites, and "En Espanol" provides Spanish language materials.

Medem–Bioterrorism
<http://www.medem.com/medlb/article_detaillb.cfm?article_ID= ZZZPF5U3WSC&sub_cat=57>

Founded by leading medical societies in the United States, Medem was created "to become the most comprehensive and trusted source of healthcare content in the Internet." Its "Bioterrorism" page provides links to several "frequently asked questions" sections that provide information on bioterrorism in general, children and bioterrorism, anthrax, and smallpox. The site also provides information about plague, viral hemorrhagic fever, and botulism. There are also links to the AMA's warning against antibiotic misuse and to an article from Medem's Editor-in-Chief entitled "Flu and Anthrax Season: How Can We Separate the Two?"

NOAH: New York Online Access to Health
<http://www.noah-health.org/>

This is a unique collection of state, local, and federal health resources for consumers. NOAH's mission is "to provide high quality full-text information for consumers that is accurate, timely, relevant and unbiased." The "Health Topics and Resources" section contains links to information about anthrax and smallpox. There is also a "Mental Health" link that leads to a section, "Dealing with Traumatic Events." Information is available in both English and Spanish, and the majority of items are provided in full text.

ELECTRONIC BOOKS

Harrison's Online: Bioterrorism Watch
<http://www.harrisonsonline.com/amed/public/amed_news/news_article/281.html>

McGraw-Hill, in collaboration with *The New England Journal of Medicine*, is providing complimentary access to relevant content from *Harrison's Online* and a link to a similar set of information at the Journal's Web site. Selected chapters from *Harrison's* are in a printable format. Chapter topics include upper respiratory tract infections, botulism, tularemia, plague, smallpox, vaccinia, and other poxviruses. There are also links to selected resources on bioterrorism and related bioterrorism news stories.

Hospital Preparedness for Mass Casualties, Final Report (August 2000)
<http://www.ahapolicyforum.org/policyresources/MOdisaster.asp>

The American Hospital Association Policy Forum, with the support of the Office of Emergency Preparedness and the U.S. Department of Health and Human Services, prepared this final report from a March 2000 meeting. Participants of this invitational forum were a diverse group of hospital and government personnel. The purpose of the forum was to develop recommendations and strategies about mass casualty preparedness for hospitals, the American Hospital Association, and the HHS Office of Emergency Preparedness. Identified needs are grouped into four areas of preparedness: community-wide, communication, public policy, and staffing.

Medical Aspects of Chemical and Biological Warfare in *Textbook of Military Medicine* (1997)
<http://www.armymedicine.army.mil/history/borden/cwbw/default.htm>

The *Textbook of Military Medicine* is a series published by the Office of the Surgeon General, Department of the Army, United States of

America. This section within the series provides a historical overview of biological warfare and a look at the threat of biological warfare. It also includes chapters on various biological agents including anthrax, smallpox, and viral hemorrhagic fevers. Information provided in the chapters includes pathogenesis, clinical manifestations, diagnosis, and treatment. The resource is available in PDF format.

USAMRIID's Medical Management of Biological Casualties Handbook (Fourth Edition, 2001)
<http://www.usamriid.army.mil/education/bluebook.html>

Published by the U.S. Army Medical Research Institute of Infectious Diseases (USAMRIID), the handbook, also known as the "Blue Book," provides basic summary and treatment information to health care professionals who need a quick reference format (see Figure 2). Major sections include "Bacterial Agents" (anthrax, plague, etc.), "Viral Agents" (smallpox, viral hemorrhagic fever, etc.), and "Biological Toxins" (botulinum, ricin, etc.). Within these sections, a one-page summary of each biological agent is followed by a more in-depth look at the agent. The summaries include information on signs and symptoms, diagnosis, treatment, prophylaxis, and isolation, and decontamination. Other sections in the handbook discuss the issues of detection, personal protection, and decontamination. The many appendices include information on medical terminology, patient isolation precautions, characteristics of agents, medical sample collection, differential diagnosis between toxins and nerve agents, and references and emergency response contacts. The resource is available in Adobe Acrobat, Palm OS, MS Word, and MS Word (with hyperlinks) formats.

Treatment of Biological Warfare Agent Casualties (July 2000)
<http://www.vnh.org/FM8284/index.html>

Published by the Headquarters Departments of The Army, The Navy, and the Air Force, and Commandant, Marine Corps, this resource was developed for members of the Armed Forces Medical Services and other medically qualified personnel. As stated in the preface, it "classifies and describes potential BW [biological warfare] agents; provides procedures for collecting, handling and labeling, shipping, and identifying potential BW agents; describes procedures for medical diagnosing, treating, and management of BW casualties; describes medical management and treatment in BW operations." The entries for individual agents in the chapters on "Bacterial Agents," "Viral Agents," and "Toxins" follow the same basic format: general information is followed

FIGURE 2. USAMRIID's Medical Management of Biological Casualties Handbook

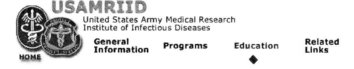

USAMRIID
United States Army Medical Research
Institute of Infectious Diseases

HOME   General Information   Programs   Education   Related Links

USAMRIID's MEDICAL MANAGEMENT
OF BIOLOGICAL CASUALTIES HANDBOOK
Fourth Edition February 2001

Section	Word	PDF
Blue Book Title and Disclaimer	Word (1 MB)	PDF (30 KB)
Introduction and Blue Book	Word (286 KB)	PDF (234 KB)
Appendix A: Glossary of Medical Terms	Word (60 KB)	PDF (33 KB)
Appendix B: Patient Isolation Precautions	Word (24 KB)	PDF (12 KB)
Appendix C: BW Agent Characteristics	Word (27 KB)	PDF (15 KB)
Appendix D: BW Agent Vaccines, Therapeutics and Prophylactics	Word (41 KB)	PDF (19 KB)
Appendix E: Medical Sample Collections for BW Agents	Word (39 KB)	PDF (21 KB)
Appendix F: Specimens for Laboratory Diagnosis	Word (22 KB)	PDF (9 KB)
Appendix G: BW Agent Laboratory Identification	Word (27 KB)	PDF (11 KB)
Appendix H: Differential Diagnosis - Toxins vs. Nerve Agents	Word (20 KB)	PDF (7 KB)
Appendix I: Comparative Lethality - Toxins vs. Chemical Agents	Word (21 KB)	PDF (9 KB)
Appendix J: Aerosol Toxicity	Word (24 KB)	PDF (7 KB)
Appendix K: References and Emergency Response Contacts	Word (107 KB)	PDF (42 KB)

1. **Palm OS Version:** (145 KB)
"MMBCH4.02.zip" is designed for Palm Pilot users to download to their handheld units. The "Read.me" file contains user instructions.

by information on biological warfare agent delivery, environmental detection, prevention, biological warfare clinical presentation, diagnosis, treatment, control of patients, contacts, treatment areas, and medical evacuation. This resource is available in HTML and PDF formats.

GOVERNMENT SITES

Centers for Disease Control and Prevention (CDC)
Public Health Emergency Preparedness & Response
<http://www.bt.cdc.gov/>

The Centers for Disease Control and Prevention, an agency of the U.S. Department of Health and Human Services, has created a Web site that provides access to anthrax and other bioterrorism information (see Figure 3). The anthrax section provides agent information intended for the health care provider and includes details about the disease, recommended treatment, specific issues relating to recognizing anthrax in emergency departments, basic laboratory protocols, and advisories.

Also on the site is an "Agents/Diseases" section that contains information on biological agents (e.g., smallpox and plague) and chemical agents. Other links lead to issues in epidemiology and surveillance, information technology, laboratory activities, law and ethics, media and health communications, and planning guidance for state and local organizations. Specific state/local project efforts associated with bioterrorism preparedness and response are profiled and a link to training information is provided.

Other links on the main page include the "United States Postal Service," "National Pharmaceutical Stockpile," the "Health Alert Network," "Videos/Satellite Broadcasts," "Health Agency Locator (HAL)," and "MMWR Information about Anthrax and Bioterrorism."

The CDC's Division of Healthcare Quality Promotion has created a collection of resources specifically for health care facilities called

FIGURE 3. Centers for Disease Control and Prevention. Public Health Emergency Preparedness & Response

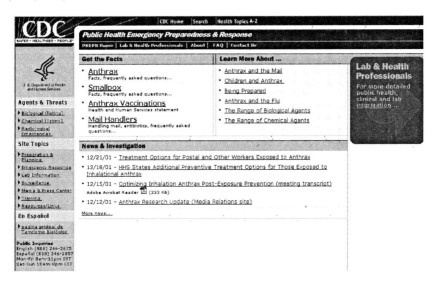

"Bioterrorism Info for Healthcare" <http://www.cdc.gov/ncidod/hip/Bio/bio.htm>. It offers fact sheets and links to resources on prevention and control, evaluation and diagnosis, laboratory protocols, and treatment. Selected information is in Spanish. Information may be in HTML, Word, or PDF format or archived broadcasts (webcasts).

Agency for Healthcare Research and Quality (AHRQ)
National Guideline Clearinghouse
Guidelines for Bioterrorism Agents
<http://www.guideline.gov/STATIC/bio.asp?view=bio>

This Web site contains evidence-based clinical practice guidelines on bioterrorism agents developed by the CDC and Johns Hopkins University Center for Civilian Biodefense Studies. Guidelines include the date of release and a statement indicating whether an update is in progress. Also included is medical management such as vaccination, therapy, post exposure prophylaxis, infection control, and decontamination. Guidelines are available in HTML and PDF formats.

Office of Homeland Security
<http://www.whitehouse.gov/homeland>

Information about the Office of Homeland Security and the Homeland Security Council are provided at this site (see Figure 4). The Office of Homeland Security is coordinating national strategy to strengthen protections against terrorist threats or attacks in the United States.

U.S. Food and Drug Administration (FDA)
Bioterrorism
<http://www.fda.gov/oc/opacom/hottopics/bioterrorism.html>

Links to information on bioterrorism from government agencies and selected academic institutions are provided at this site. Included are resources on biological agents, drug treatments, public health initiatives, preparedness, food safety, news items, and FAQs on bioterrorism.

U.S. Department of Health and Human Services
Anthrax and Biological Incidents: Preparedness and Response
<http://www.hhs.gov/hottopics/healing/biological.html>

This site provides links to information regarding the department's role in emergency preparedness and response in the event of a biologi-

FIGURE 4. Office of Homeland Security

cal or other public health emergency. Resources include government information on anthrax and smallpox. Of special value are links to the full text of testimony and speeches on bioterrorism. Selected information is in Spanish.

ORGANIZATIONS

The American College of Physicians (ACP) and the American Society of Internal Medicine (ASIM) ACP-ASIM Online's Bioterrorism Resource <http://www.acponline.org/bioterro/>

ACP-ASIM Online's Bioterrorism Resource page has a wealth of information resources aimed at the physician. In addition to general and introductory information about bioterrorism, the site includes physicians' decision support tools, medical information on specific biologic agents, online bioterrorism courses, information for patients, information for institutions, and news. Included is an alphabetical list of experts in the field, which serves as a bioterrorism speakers' bureau. A search feature enables physicians to search for FBI field offices and public health offices by state. A version of the site is available for PalmOS PDA users.

American Medical Association
Disaster Preparedness and Medical Response
<http://www.ama-assn.org/ama/pub/category/6206.html>

The mission of the American Medical Association (AMA)'s Disaster Preparedness and Medical Response Web page is to educate physicians to recognize and respond to biological attacks. It includes sections on "News from AMA Member Communications," "AMA Resources," "Physician Resources," "Federal Resources," "Coping with Disaster," and "National and State Resources." "AMA Resources" includes FAQs on biologic agents and provides links to the AMA's Council on Scientific Affairs reports on terrorism. The AMA's 55th Interim Meeting (December 1-5, 2001) devoted a major portion of its content to bioterrorism. Look for this site to offer Webcasts of the educational sessions provided for physicians from the Interim Meeting. The site offers the AMA's *Bioterrorism Agents Quick Reference Guide* and selected full-text articles from *JAMA, New England Journal of Medicine,* and *American Journal of Public Health.* It also provides links to *JAMA* consensus statements on anthrax, botulinum toxin, plague, smallpox, and tularemia used as biological weapons.

btresponse.org–resources for medical professionals
<http://www.btresponse.org>

The American Academy of Family Physicians has created this site with sponsorship from the Association of Medical Publications. The goal of the site is to "help medical professionals prepare for and respond to bioterrorism and other threats." The site links to the latest bioterrorism updates, articles from *MMWR* and other journals, patient education materials, information about biological, chemical and nuclear weapons, and resources on post-disaster mental health concerns.

Center for Civilian Biodefense Studies, Johns Hopkins University
<http://www.hopkins-biodefense.org/>

The Center is a joint entity of the Johns Hopkins University Schools of Public Health and Medicine and is sponsored by the Alfred P. Sloan and the Robert Wood Johnson Foundations. The Center's Web site (see

Figure 5) provides links to a variety of resources dealing with bioterrorism including the consensus statements for anthrax, botulinum toxin, plague, smallpox, and tularemia published in *JAMA*; the *Hopkins Antibiotic Guide* that provides diagnostic criteria and treatment guidelines for anthrax, botulism, smallpox and plague; a FAQ section for the general public; fact sheets that provide background information on various biological agents; and links to the special section, "Confronting Biological Weapons," in *Clinical Infectious Diseases.* The site also has a section on current anthrax information that includes a primer for physicians, selected medical case studies from the literature, a "frequently asked questions" section dealing with environmental detection of anthrax, and an information link for physicians with a list of "frequently asked ques-

FIGURE 5. Center for Civilian Biodefense Studies, Johns Hopkins University

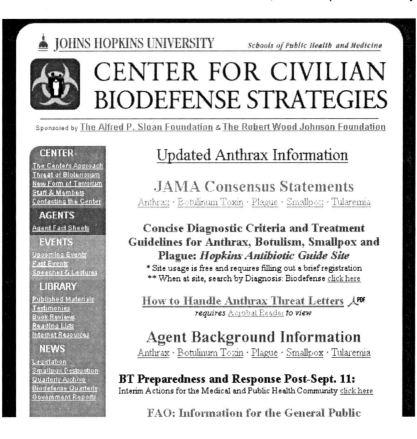

tions" related to clinical issues of anthrax infection. Information may be in HTML or PDF format.

National Association of County and City Health Officials (NACCHO)
Bioterrorism and Emergency Response Program
<http://www.naccho.org/project63.cfm>

NACCHO, in collaboration with local, state, and federal partners, is involved in programs to strengthen and improve local health agencies' capacity to respond to bioterrorism. This Web site consists of three major topical areas. The "Bioterrorism Performance Standards" section provides information to assist communities in assessing their capacity to respond to bioterrorist disease threats. "Local Centers for Public Health Preparedness" includes links to best practices and offers models for strengthening public health capacity. "Preparedness and Response to Chemical and Biological Terrorism" includes a link to *Elements of Effective Bioterrorism Preparedness*, a document designed to assist local public health officials in identifying their public health and safety roles when responding to bioterrorism. Some information has distribution restrictions. NACCHO staff must be contacted directly for selected fact sheets and background papers.

StatePublicHealth.org
<http://www.statepublichealth.org/index.php>

For information about local responses to bioterrorism access state public health Web sites. StatePublicHealth.org, a product of the Association of State and Territorial Health Officials (ASTHO) and ASTHO affiliates, provides links to directories of state health agencies, state health officials, and public hotlines. Under "Search Related Public Health Sites," enter a phrase to search for a topic in a variety of public health sites.

REFERENCES

1. "Backgrounder: Terrorism." Federal Emergency Management Agency (FEMA). Available: <http://www.fema.gov/library/terror.htm>. Accessed: January 2, 2002.

2. "Recognition of Illness Associated with the Intentional Release of a Biologic Agent." *MMWR Weekly*, October 19, 2001, Available: <http://www.cdc.gov/mmwr/preview/mmwrhtml/mm5041a2.htm>. Accessed: January 4, 2002.

3. "Update: Investigation of Bioterrorism-related Anthrax, 2001." *MMWR Weekly*, November 16, 2001, Available: <http://www.cdc.gov/mmwr/preview/mmwrhtml/mm5045a2.htm>. Accessed: January 4, 2002.

4. "Update: Investigation of Bioterrorism-related Anthrax and Adverse Events from Antimicrobial Prophylaxis." *MMWR Weekly*, November 9, 2001, Available: <http://www.cdc.gov/mmwr/preview/mmwrhtml/mm5044a1.htm>. Accessed: January 4, 2002.

5. Bettina M. Stopford. "Responding to the Threat of Bioterrorism: Practical Resources and References, and the Importance of Preparation." *Journal of Emergency Nursing* 27, no. 5 (October 2001): 471-475, 521-526.

6. H. Clifford Lane and Anthony S. Fauci. "Bioterrorism in the Home Front: A New Challenge for American Medicine." *JAMA* 286, no. 20 (November 28, 2001): 2595-2597.

Anthrax Resources on the Web

Edwin A. Holtum
Linda K. Roth

SUMMARY. The recent anthrax cases and anthrax scares in the United States have prompted understandable interest and concern on the part of health professionals, officials, and the public. This interest comprises virtually all aspects of the disease including its possible methods of transmission (both natural and intentional), varying disease forms, diagnosis, symptoms, therapy, and prevention. With the possibility of future criminal or terrorist anthrax attacks on a larger scale now a realistic threat, members of the public are also rightly interested in national and global measures to prevent and defend against such attacks and wish to keep abreast of these efforts as they unfold. This article describes the onset of the present crisis, a brief description of the disease, some of the current efforts to deal with it, and selected Web sites that the authors consider particularly comprehensive, accurate, authoritative, reliable, up-to-date, and user-friendly. *[Article copies available for a fee from The Haworth Document Delivery Service: 1-800-HAWORTH. E-mail address: <getinfo@haworthpressinc.com> Website: <http://www.HaworthPress.com> © 2002 by The Haworth Press, Inc. All rights reserved.]*

KEYWORDS. Anthrax, anthrax vaccines, bioterrorism, Internet

Edwin A. Holtum (edwin-holtum@uiowa.edu) is Coordinator for Administrative and Access Services and Linda K. Roth (linda-roth@uiowa.edu) is Library Assistant IV and Web Developer, both at Hardin Library for the Health Sciences, University of Iowa, Iowa City, IA 52242.

[Haworth co-indexing entry note]: "Anthrax Resources on the Web." Holtum, Edwin A., and Linda K. Roth. Co-published simultaneously in *Internet Reference Services Quarterly* (The Haworth Information Press, an imprint of The Haworth Press, Inc.) Vol. 6, No. 3/4, 2002, pp. 17-31; and: *Bioterrorism and Political Violence: Web Resources* (ed: M. Sandra Wood) The Haworth Information Press, an imprint of The Haworth Press, Inc., 2002, pp. 17-31. Single or multiple copies of this article are available for a fee from The Haworth Document Delivery Service [1-800-HAWORTH, 9:00 a.m. - 5:00 p.m. (EST). E-mail address: getinfo@haworthpressinc.com].

INTRODUCTION

On September 18, 2001, one week after the horrific attacks on the World Trade Center and Pentagon, envelopes containing a then unknown substance were sent from Trenton, New Jersey to the headquarters of NBC News and the New York Post. Several days later, when blisters appeared on the fingers of an editorial page assistant at the New York Post, the granular substance was positively identified to contain anthrax bacteria. Subsequent cutaneous anthrax infections in mail handlers and office workers caused widespread concern among the American public who, rightly, suspected criminal intent. This fear was greatly intensified when on October 3, 2001, a Florida photo editor from American Media, Inc. (AMI), in Boca Raton was diagnosed with inhalation anthrax, the deadliest of the Anthrax forms. The editor died two days later, thus becoming the first U.S. anthrax fatality in 25 years. In the weeks that followed, anthrax appeared in other AMI employees, and company headquarters were abandoned on October 16. Meanwhile, a day earlier, a letter sent to U.S. Senate Majority Leader Tom Daschle tested positive for anthrax. On October 17, after 28 House of Representative workers tested positive for anthrax exposure, the House Office Building was shut down.[1]

As anthrax cases and anthrax-laced letters and documents continued to surface around New York and Washington, D.C. (including Capitol Hill), the FBI still had no clues as to the identity or motives of the criminals. At this writing, the anthrax outbreaks have resulted in 12 cases of cutaneous anthrax and 11 cases (including five deaths) of inhalation anthrax.[2]

While the number of victims remains relatively small, the potential threat of anthrax as a weapon of bioterrorism continues to worry officials and the public; the media have devoted enormous coverage to the issue. And although, for a variety of reasons, anthrax spores would be very difficult to distribute on a massive level, a Congressional analysis estimated that between 130,000 and 3 million deaths could result if the means were found to release 100 kilograms of anthrax spores over Washington, D.C.[3]

Anthrax is caused by the *Bacillus anthracis* bacteria and is usually transmitted to humans who have had contact with animals or animal products that contain bacterial spores. Until the recent criminal attacks, anthrax was largely eradicated in Europe and North America, although it remains a threat to both animals and humans in developing countries that lack adequate countermeasures and where soil conditions are especially conducive to long-term spore survival. Cattle are especially susceptible to the systemic form of anthrax, which usually claims its victims within 24 to 48 hours.

Humans are susceptible to three forms of anthrax: cutaneous, inhalation, and gastrointestinal. The last form is virtually unknown in North America. Cutaneous anthrax is, by far, the most common and is spread as anthrax spores come in contact with sores or open wounds. The toxins in the bacteria result in tissue death which, in turn, lead to the development of an extensive black scab (the name anthrax is derived from the Greek word for coal) which is usually painless. The mortality rate for cutaneous anthrax is around 25% when left untreated. However, the overall mortality rate is much lower owing to its good response to treatment.

Inhalation anthrax, although uncommon, is the deadlier form of the disease and is contracted by the inhalation of tiny anthrax spores, which eventually reach the lymph nodes where massive hemorrhaging can result. The cause of death is usually respiratory failure, pulmonary edema, or shock with death occurring within one or two days of acute symptoms.

Gastrointestinal anthrax has never been reported in the United States but does occur in developing countries. Symptoms include stomach pains and diarrhea. Toxemia and shock may then occur, often leading to death. Often the disease goes undiagnosed until after death.[4]

Numerous antibiotics are effective in treating anthrax. Most of the recent victims and those feared exposed to the disease were given ciproflaxacin (U.S. trade name, Cipro). CNN reported in late October 2001 that over 10,000 people in the Washington, D.C. area were taking the drug.[5] Recently, however, public health officials have encouraged the use of other antibiotics, most notably, doxycycline, which is equally effective and less expensive. In addition, there is a danger of antibiotic resistance occurring when a single drug is used over a long period of time. This is also the reason why physicians are being discouraged from prescribing either drug except in cases of exposure or where a definite diagnosis has been made.

Under normal circumstances, the anthrax vaccine (designed in the 1950s and 1960s and FDA approved in 1970) is used in the United States in highly selective circumstances, primarily in workers whose occupations require working with imported animal hides and furs. In 1998, however, controversy arose when the Secretary of Defense approved a vaccination plan designed to inoculate all military personnel by the year 2003. Many soldiers complained of side effects and over

100 individuals have now faced court martial for refusing to be inoculated. Since the recent threats, various scientific teams have been moving quickly to develop a new anthrax vaccine that will prove more effective with less side effects. The challenge is complicated by the fact that there are over 1,000 known anthrax strains and the vaccine needs to be effective against all of them. To date, the U.S. government has no plans for a wide scale inoculation program for the general population, and it is unlikely such a program would be put into place short of a more critical risk.[6]

On October 28, 2001, President Bush signed an executive order establishing the Office of Homeland Security and the Homeland Security Council. Much of the work of this Executive Body has to do with coordinating efforts among the many federal agencies whose work involves bioterrorism. In late November, the U.S. Postal Service announced it would begin irradiating mail as a countermeasure against anthrax-laden mail. The systems, to be installed at post offices throughout the country use high voltage electron beams to kill bacteria.[7] The plan has drawn some criticism from consumer groups concerned with worker safety. Other preventive measures have included the institution of higher security levels at local and national government laboratories.

As one would expect, the number of Internet sites relating to anthrax has grown dramatically over the past few months. An AltaVista search revealed a threefold growth of anthrax related sites from September 1 to November 1, 2001. Virtually all major health related public and private agencies and organizations have added information on anthrax or have added links to relevant sites. While most of this information is reliable, it will come as no surprise that there are scores of additional sites containing misleading and false information as well as sites that include bogus offers of detection and protection. The difficulty is not finding information on anthrax but finding reliable, honest, and up-to-date information. Shortly after the reports about anthrax exposure in the United States came in, Dr. Gro Harlem Brundtland, Director-General of the World Health Organization said, "There are three lessons from recent events: first, public health systems have responded promptly to the suspicion of deliberate infections; second, these systems must continue to be vigilant; and third, an informed and responsible public is a critical part of the response."[8] This guide has been assembled in the hope that it will play a part in furthering the last of these lessons.

CONSUMER HEALTH RESOURCES

MEDLINEplus: Anthrax
<http://www.nlm.nih.gov/medlineplus/anthrax.html>

MEDLINEplus: Biological & Chemical Weapons
<http://www.nlm.nih.gov/medlineplus/
biologicalandchemicalweapons.html>

MEDLINEplus, developed and designed by the National Library of Medicine as an authoritative resource for health information for both professionals and the public, is perhaps the single best site from which to launch an Internet search on anthrax. This highly respected and comprehensive resource uses primary information from the National Institutes of Health as well as other respected sources, including the MEDLINE database. The pages on anthrax and biological and chemical weapons include the latest news, overviews, prevention and screening, research, treatment (including alternative therapies) as well as links to information for children. Some Spanish language information is provided as well.

Of special note is an interactive tutorial from the Patient Education Institute that provides an excellent introduction to anthrax for the general public. The site also provides an automated up-to-date search for anthrax or biological and chemical weapons from the MEDLINE database.

NOAH (New York Online Access to Health): Anthrax
<http://www.noah-health.org/english/illness/infect/anthrax.html>

"NOAH aims to provide the public with high quality health information in English and Spanish that is specifically geared for the consumer." Originally funded by the U.S. Department of Commerce, it is now sponsored by a variety of public and private organizations, including the New York Public Library. It is one of the first consumer-oriented health sites and remains one of the finest. The anthrax section includes links to both government and private resources, including the major news groups (see Figure 1). There are special sections for children and teens as well as information on anthrax and pregnancy and how the disease may affect children differently than adults.

FIGURE 1. NOAH: Anthrax

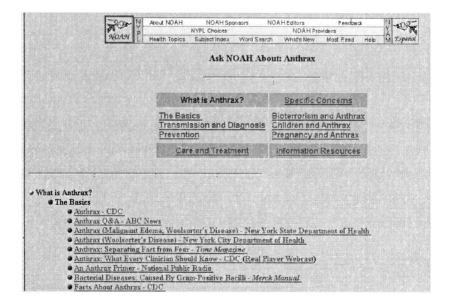

Healthfinder: Anthrax and Bioterrorism
<http://www.healthfinder.gov/anthrax_bioterrorism.htm>

Developed by the U.S. Department of Health and Human Services, in collaboration with other federal agencies, Healthfinder is primarily geared to directing consumers to appropriate government links, though some private resources are included as well. Included in the anthrax/bioterrorism section are links to Webcasts, CDC advisories, and FAQs from a variety of sources. Especially notable is the extensive list of Spanish language links.

GOVERNMENT SITES

Centers for Disease Control and Prevention (CDC)
Public Health Emergency Preparedness & Response: Anthrax
<http://www.bt.cdc.gov/Agent/Anthrax/Anthrax.asp>

The CDC, an agency of the Department of Health and Human Services, is the leading federal agency in charge of protecting the nation's health and safety. The CDC site is the most authoritative site for anthrax information.

The site provides extensive information about anthrax primarily for medical and public health care providers and officials, laboratory workers, environmental and industrial hygiene professionals, firefighters, and other emergency responders but also includes information for the general public. The information is provided in a variety of formats including an extensive frequently asked questions page, fact sheets, archives of Webcasts, training materials for public health workers, news items, pages written in Spanish and links to other Anthrax sites.

The CDC anthrax page is broken down into the following categories:

- Agent Information–designed for health care providers, this section includes information about anthrax including recommendations for identification and treatment
- Clinical Level-A Lab Protocol–designed for laboratories, this section includes protocols for identifying microorganisms to aid clinicians in their diagnosis of anthrax
- News & Media–this section includes CDC news releases, advisories, and links to archived Web broadcasts providing information for laboratory workers, clinicians, and infection control workers.

Morbidity and Mortality Weekly Report (MMWR) Information About Anthrax and Bioterrorism <http://www.cdc.gov/mmwr/indexbt.html>

The *MMWR* is prepared by the CDC based on weekly reports by state health departments. Since the death of a Florida man from inhalation anthrax was reported in early October 2001, the MMWR has published numerous articles about anthrax including guidelines and recommendations concerning diagnosis and treatment, distinguishing influenza-like illness from inhalation anthrax, the use of antimicrobial prophylaxis in persons exposed to anthrax, reports of adverse effects of antibiotics use among postal workers, and much more. Anthrax articles published prior to October 2001 as well as other bioterrorism related articles from the MMWR are also included on this page.

United States Postal Service (USPS): Security of the Mail <http://www.usps.com/news/2001/press/serviceupdates.htm>

This site provides information for businesses, postal employees, and the general public about the USPS's efforts to keep the mail safe. It includes training modules for mail centers, mailroom safety video clips, fact sheets, news releases, and information about state and local mail facilities. Posters and postcards used to identify suspicious letters or packages can be downloaded and printed from this site.

U.S. Food and Drug Administration (FDA): Bioterrorism
<http://www.fda.gov/oc/opacom/hottopics/bioterrorism.html>

The FDA has as one of its many responsibilities the monitoring of the safety of drugs. Included in its bioterrorism site is information about Cipro (ciprofloxacin hydrochloride) and doxycycline, the antibiotics used to treat inhalation anthrax. The site also provides information about buying medications online, antibiotic resistance, and the anthrax vaccine.

Occupational Safety & Health Administration (OSHA)
Protecting the Worksite Against Terrorism: Anthrax
<http://www.osha.gov/bioterrorism/anthrax/>

OSHA's mission is to ensure the safety of America's workers. OSHA's anthrax site includes "Workplace Response to Anthrax Threat: OSHA Recommendations for Handling Mail," "How Can You Prevent/Control Exposure and Infection?", "Anthrax in the Workplace: Risk Reduction Matrix," plus links to other government agencies and organizations involved with anthrax issues (see Figure 2).

U.S. Fire Administration/Federal Emergency Management Agency
<http://www.usfa.fema.gov/hazmat/bioagents.htm>

The U.S. Fire Administration provides an "Anthrax Information Resources for First Responders" page which includes a variety of recommendations and guidelines including the selection and use of protective clothing, handling anthrax threats, and the clinical evaluation of persons with possible anthrax.

Anthrax Vaccine Immunization Program (AVIP) Agency
of the Office of the Army Surgeon General,
Department of Defense
<http://www.anthrax.osd.mil/>

This site contains information concerning the many issues surrounding the anthrax vaccine. Designed primarily for military personnel, the

FIGURE 2. OSHA. Protecting the Worksite Against Terrorism: Anthrax

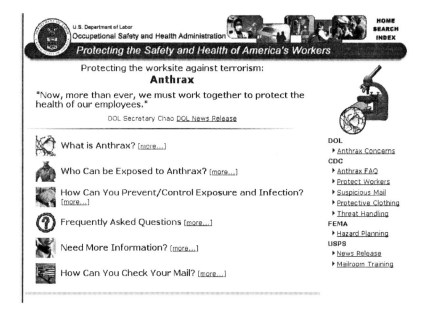

site includes descriptions of the disease and the vaccine, production and safety issues of the vaccine, reader mail, links to other organizations and agencies, and bibliographies.

This site includes "Situation Report: Anthrax" <http://www.anthrax. osd.mil/HTML_interface/default.html> with updated information about the number of confirmed and suspected cases of inhalation and cutaneous anthrax in the U.S., recent news reports, guidelines, recommendations, and historical information. Also included is a link to the full text of the *Science* article "The Sverdlovsk Anthrax Outbreak of 1979," which describes the accidental release of anthrax spores from a Soviet military microbiology facility and the resulting deaths of at least 68 people.

The U.S. Army Medical Research Institute of Infectious Diseases (USAMRIID)
<http://www.usamriid.army.mil/>

USAMRIID is the Department of Defense's lead laboratory for medical aspects of biological warfare defense.

Medical NBC Online Information Server
<http://www.nbc-med.org>

The Medical NBC (Nuclear, Biological and Chemical) Online Information Server is provided as a public service of the U.S. Army's Office of the Surgeon General.

The Office of Homeland Security
<http://www.whitehouse.gov/homeland/>

This site provides information about the Office of Homeland Security and the Homeland Security Council and includes the latest developments on the fight against terrorism.

JOURNALS/BOOKS

Following the initial anthrax deaths in the fall of 2001 many journal and book publishers provided no-cost Web access to anthrax related articles and book chapters. This information often appeared weeks before the expected print publication date.

American Medical Association (AMA): Bioterrorism Articles
<http://pubs.ama-assn.org/bioterr.html>

The AMA site includes bioterrorism articles published in its flagship journal, *Journal of the American Medical Association* (*JAMA*) as well as its numerous "Archives" titles. The often-cited article "Anthrax as a Biological Weapon–Medical and Public Health Management" is a consensus statement published in *JAMA* by members of the Working Group on Civilian Biodefense. This consensus statement offers recommendations about the diagnosis and treatment of anthrax, the use of antibiotics and anthrax vaccine, environmental issues, and suggestions for additional research.

The AMA also maintains a list of full-text bioterrorism articles from other publishers <http://www.ama-assn.org/ama/pub/category/6232.html>.

Other full-text articles and book chapters:

Nature: Focus on Anthrax
<http://www.nature.com/nature/anthrax/>

New England Journal of Medicine: Special Notice: Information
About Anthrax and Other Biologic Threats
<http://nejm.org/specialnotice/>

Emerging Infectious Diseases
<http://www.cdc.gov/ncidod/EID/index.htm>

Emerging Infectious Diseases, a monthly peer-reviewed journal published by the National Center for Infectious Diseases, Centers for Disease Control and Prevention, was established "to promote the recognition of new and reemerging infectious diseases around the world and improve the understanding of factors involved in disease emergence, prevention, and elimination."

E-Medicine: Anthrax Resources
<http://www.emedicine.com/anthrax_resources.htm>

New Scientist: Bioterrorism and Bioweapons Special Report
<http://www.newscientist.com/hottopics/bioterrorism/>

Harrison's Online: Bioterrorism Watch
<http://www.harrisonsonline.com/amed/public/amed_news/news_
article/281.html>

Includes the section on Anthrax from Chapter 141, "Diphtheria, Other Corynebacterial Infections, and Anthrax" of the *Harrison's Principles of Internal Medicine* (15th edition, New York: McGraw-Hill) <http://www.mheducation.com/HOL2_chapters/HOL_chapters/chapter141.htm>.

Merck Manual of Diagnosis and Therapy, 17th edition,
Chapter 157: Bacterial Diseases
<http://www.merck.com/pubs/mmanual/section13/chapter157/157
c.htm#terrorism>

The section on anthrax was updated from the printed version in October 2001.

ORGANIZATIONS AND AGENCIES

Center for Civilian Biodefense Studies from the Johns Hopkins University Schools of Public Health and Medicine
<http://www.hopkins-biodefense.org/>

The mission of the privately funded Center for Civilian Biodefense Studies is to gather information concerning all aspects of biological terrorism, to develop recommendations, and to disseminate these recommendations to the medical and public health communities. This site includes "Clinical Anthrax: Primer for Physicians," "Case Studies of Bioterrorism-Related Inhalational Anthrax," "Environmental Detection of Anthrax–FAQ," "Anthrax Information for Clinicians," "How to Handle Anthrax Threat Letters," and much more.

This site also has a link to the Johns Hopkins Division of Infectious Diseases Antiobiotic Guide <http://www.hopkins-abxguide.org/>, a tool for clinicians that provides "concise, digested, timely information about the diagnosis and treatment of infectious diseases." Registration is required but site usage is free.

American Medical Association (AMA)
<http://www.ama-assn.org/ama/pub/category/6206.html>

In addition to the freely available articles from the AMA journals mentioned above, the AMA site provides a "Disaster Preparedness and Medical Response" site which includes links to the "AMA Message to Physicians on Anthrax" and the "AMA Warns Against Antibiotic Misuse." The site also includes an extensive directory of AMA and outside anthrax resources dealing with a variety of topics including psychosocial issues, news, physician and physician reservists resources, and links to federal, national, and state organizations.

World Health Organization
<http://www.who.int/emc/deliberate_epi.html>

The World Health Organization, a specialized agency of the United Nations, includes on its "Health Aspects of Biological & Chemical Weapons" page links to an anthrax fact sheet, a frequently asked questions section called "Guidance on Anthrax," and the monograph "Guidelines for the Surveillance and Control of Anthrax in Human and Animals."

An interesting site from the World Health Organization Collaborating Center at the School of Veterinary Medicine, Louisiana State University, is the World Anthrax Data Site <http://www.vetmed.lsu.edu/whocc/mp_world.htm>. By clicking on an area of a world map, users can determine the number of animal and human cases of anthrax reported in any given country since the late 1980s.

Center for Nonproliferation Studies (CNS)
<http://cns.miis.edu/index.htm>

CNS is the largest nongovernmental organization in the United States devoted exclusively to research and training on nonproliferation issues.

Center for the Study of Bioterrorism & Emerging Infections
Saint Louis University School of Public Health
<http://bioterrorism.slu.edu/>

This site provides fact sheets, bibliographies, slide presentations, and education and training resources on bioterrorism issues including anthrax.

Infectious Diseases Society of America
IDSA and Bioterrorism Preparedness
<http://www.idsociety.org/PA/PS&P/BT_Preparedness_10-2-01.htm>

This site provides information for infectious disease specialists and other health care providers.

Federation of American Scientists: Chemical & Biological Arms Control Program
<http://www.fas.org/bwc/>

The FAS Chemical & Biological Arms Control Program is concerned with all aspects of chemical and biological weapons. This site includes the text of articles from the popular press, the text of and information about the Biological Weapons Convention, information about agricultural bioterrorism, and more.

MORE INTERNET SITES

Hardin Meta Directory of Internet Health Sources (Hardin MD): Anthrax & Anthrax Vaccine
<http://www.lib.uiowa.edu/hardin/md/anthrax.html>

Hardin MD is a "list of lists." It includes "one-stop-shopping" sites, such as MedWeb and Yahoo, subject directories such as the Open Directory Project and Academic Info, and also independent discipline specific lists. The "Anthrax & Anthrax Vaccine" page also includes consumer health sites such as NOAH, MEDLINEplus, and Healthfinder; library or library related sites such as OCLC Online Computer Library Center, Inc. and the Librarians' Index to the Internet; U.S. government sites; and many other resources (see Figure 3).

FIGURE 3. Hardin MD: Anthrax & Anthrax Vaccine

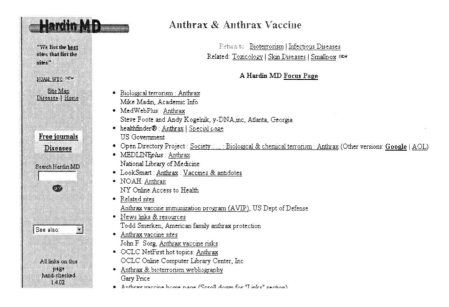

REFERENCES

1. South Florida Sun-Sentinal.com, "Chronology of Anthrax Events." Available: <http://www.sun-sentinel.com/news/local/southflorida/sfl-1013anthraxchronology.story>. Accessed: December 19, 2001.

2. Canadian Press, "Anthrax Attacks Helps Medicine Rewrite the Book on Deadly Disease," December 9, 2001. Available: <http://www.nlm.nih.gov/medlineplus/news/fullstory_5142.html >. Accessed: December 10, 2001.

3. CBC News, "Anthrax," October 2001. Available: <http://www.cbc.ca/news/indepth/background/anthrax.html>. Accessed: December 10, 2001.

4. Jonas A. Shulman, "Anthrax," Chapter 350 in *Cecil Textbook of Mmedicine*, edited by Lee Goldman. Philadelphia: W.B. Saunders, 2000.

5. CNN.com/Health, "Doxycycline Becomes Anthrax Drug of Choice in Washington," October 28, 2001. Available: <http://www.cnn.com/2001/HEALTH/conditions/10/27/doxycycline/index.html>. Accessed: December 19, 2001.

6 Laura Johannes and Laurie McGinley, "Search for Better Antrhax Vaccine Increases," *Wall Street Journal*, October 19, 2001. Available: <http://www.anthraxvaccine.org/johannes.html>. Available: December 10, 2001.

7 United States Postal Service press release, "United States Postal Service; How We're Making the Public and Employees Safe," October 29, 2001. Available: <http://www.usps.com/news/2001/press/pr01_1029steps.htm>. Accessed: December 10, 2001.

8. World Organization press release, "World Health Organization Stresses Need for Continued Public Vigilance in Responding to Deliberate Infections," October 18, 2001. Available: <http://www.who.int/disease-outbreak-news/n2001/october/18october2001.html>. Accessed: December 10, 2001.

Information for Immunity:
Internet Resources on Biological Agents
as Terrorist Weapons

Garry J. Forger
Janet A. Knight

SUMMARY. Before September 2001, bioterrorism was a term that appeared occasionally in the news, but usually only in reference to foreign wars and conflicts, or in relation to an obscure possible threat. After anthrax spores began to be mailed to offices and agencies in October of 2001, the threat was no longer an abstraction, but a reality. As the Internet has become a ubiquitous resource, authoritative agencies and organizations have used the Internet as the quickest way to provide information on bioterrorism to the general public and to planning agencies. This article provides a starting point for searching for bioterrorism information and is by no means an exhaustive list. *[Article copies available for a fee from The Haworth Document Delivery Service: 1-800-HAWORTH. E-mail address: <getinfo@haworthpressinc.com> Website: <http://www.HaworthPress. com> © 2002 by The Haworth Press, Inc. All rights reserved.]*

KEYWORDS. Bioterrorism, biological agents, biological weapons, chemical weapons, Internet

---

Garry J. Forger (gforger@u.arizona.edu) is Academic Data Specialist and Janet A. Knight (jknight@u.arizona.edu) is Senior Research Specialist, both at the University of Arizona, Office of Distributed Learning, 1077 North Highland Avenue, Tucson, AZ 85721-0073.

[Haworth co-indexing entry note]: "Information for Immunity: Internet Resources on Biological Agents as Terrorist Weapons." Forger, Garry J., and Janet A. Knight. Co-published simultaneously in *Internet Reference Services Quarterly* (The Haworth Information Press, an imprint of The Haworth Press, Inc.) Vol. 6, No. 3/4, 2002, pp. 33-45; and: *Bioterrorism and Political Violence: Web Resources* (ed: M. Sandra Wood) The Haworth Information Press, an imprint of The Haworth Press, Inc., 2002, pp. 33-45. Single or multiple copies of this article are available for a fee from The Haworth Document Delivery Service [1-800-HAWORTH, 9:00 a.m. - 5:00 p.m. (EST). E-mail address: getinfo@haworthpressinc.com].

33

INTRODUCTION

Before September 2001, bioterrorism was a term that appeared occasionally in the news, but usually only in reference to foreign wars and conflicts, or in relation to an obscure possible threat. After anthrax spores began to be mailed to offices and agencies in October of 2001, the threat was no longer an abstraction, but a reality. In the face of this new reality more questions began to be raised about bioterrorism and more in depth inquiries began to take place on the threats and realities of bioterrorism. Some of the frustrations that both consumers and professionals found, as they began to try and make sense of the threat, are illustrated by the search results found by searching Google. Searching Google for "bioterrorism" results in 233,000 hits, searching for "biological weapons" results in 179,000 hits and narrowing the search to "bioterrorism (consumer or health or prevention)" still brings back 145,000 hits.

Further investigation reveals that "bioterrorism" is an all encompassing term that refers to an entire panoply of biological and chemical agents that vary in their ability to be used as weapons and that require a wide range of types of defense. Believing that information is the best defense, this article will attempt to define some of the things that make up "bioterrorism" and will provide links to Internet resources that can be used to obtain more information. These specific examples provide an overview of the types of agents and chemicals that can and have been used as terrorist weapons. To answer questions on consumer health, public health, and public preparedness included here are Web sites where more information can be located. State and local health departments may also have information available on bioterrorism preparedness.

CATEGORIES OF BIOTERRORISM

Bioterrorism can be divided into the two broad categories of biological agents and chemical agents. Biological agents can be classified as falling into one of the following categories: bacterial, fungal, viral, or toxins. The method of disseminating each of these types of agents varies, as does defense and treatment. Included here is a single example of each of these categories of biological and chemical weapons.

Bacteria

Illinois Department of Public Health–Healthbeat
<http://www.idph.state.il.us/public/hb/hbtulare.htm>

Bacteria are single-celled microorganisms which can exist either as independent (free-living) organisms or as parasites depending on another organism for life. Bacterial infections can usually be treated with antibiotics. An example of bacteria is Tularemia. Tularemia is one of the most infectious pathogenic bacteria known, and humans as well as animals can become infected. Also known as rabbit fever, Tularemia can be spread to humans by contact with tissue or blood of infected animals, through deer flies or ticks, eating insufficiently cooked rabbit meat, drinking water, inhaling contaminated dust from soil, and contaminated pelts or paws of animals. Tularemia cannot be spread from person to person. Symptoms can include swollen lymph nodes, ulcerated skin, pneumonia-like illness, sore throat, abdominal pain, diarrhea, and vomiting. The threat of Tularemia as a weapon is greatest as an aerosol agent. Antibiotics are available for treating Tularemia.

Fungi

Coccidiosis: Diagnosis,Treatment, and Prevention
<http://beaglesunlimited.com/beaglehealth_coccidiosis.htm>

Fungus is a plantlike organism that feeds on organic matter. An example of a common fungus is the yeast organism which causes thrush and diaper rash. An example of a fungi that can affect humans is *Coccidiosis. Coccidiosis* is an intestinal disease that affects several different animal species including canines and humans. *Coccidia* is one of the most prevalent protozoal infections in North American animals, second only to *giardia.* Some species cause diseases that result in mild symptoms that might go unnoticed (i.e., mild diarrhea) and eventually disappear, while other species cause highly virulent infections that are rapidly fatal. The causative agent is a protozoan that has the ability to multiply rapidly. The potential use of this as a bioterrorist weapon may be greater for animals than humans.

Virus

Travel Medicine: Viral Hemorrhagic Fevers
<http://www.methodisthealth.com/travel/viral.htm>

A virus is a microorganism that is smaller than bacteria, which cannot grow or reproduce apart from a living cell. A virus invades a living cell and uses the cell's chemical makeup to survive and to reproduce. Viruses cause many common human infections, and are also responsible for a multitude of rare diseases. Examples of viral illnesses range from the common cold, which is usually caused by one of the rhinoviruses, to acquired immunodeficiency syndrome (AIDS), which is caused by the human immunodeficiency virus (HIV). An example of a viral infection is Viral hemorrhagic fevers (VHF). VHF is a term that refers to a group of illnesses caused by several distinct families of viruses. While some types of hemorrhagic fever viruses cause illnesses that are relatively mild, many of these cause severe, life-threatening diseases with no known cures. VHFs can be aerosolized and could be used as a biological weapon. VHFs can be transmitted from human to human, and there is no known cure or drug treatment for these diseases.

Toxins

CDC Disease Informatio–Botulism
<http://www.cdc.gov/ncidod/dbmd/diseaseinfo/botulism_g.htm>

The term "toxin" is frequently used to refer specifically to a particular protein produced by some higher plants, animals, and pathogenic (disease-causing) bacteria. A toxin typically is highly poisonous to living creatures. Toxins can be distinguished from chemical weapons in that they are naturally occurring, as opposed to being manufactured. An example of a toxin is Botulism. Botulism is a rare but serious paralytic illness caused by a nerve toxin that is produced by the bacterium *Clostridium botulinum*. The symptoms of botulism include double or blurred vision, drooping eyelids, slurred speech, difficulty swallowing, dry mouth, and muscle weakness. Muscle paralysis can also be caused by bacterial toxin. If untreated, these symptoms may progress to cause paralysis of the arms, legs, trunk, and respiratory muscles. As a weapon, botulinum toxins may be aerosolized or used to sabotage food supplies.

Chemical Terrorism

Chemical Weapons Convention–Mustard Agents
<http://www.opcw.nl/chemhaz/mustard.htm>

Chemical agents that could be used by terrorists include poisonous gases, liquids, or solids that can have toxic effects on people, animals, or plants. Most chemical agents are capable of causing serious injuries or death. The severity of injuries depends on the type and amount of the chemical agent used, and the duration of exposure. An example of a chemical weapon that has been used in war is Mustard Gas. Mustard agent is very simple to manufacture and can cause injury to the respiratory system even in concentrations which are so low that the human sense of smell cannot distinguish them. In the form of gas or liquid, mustard agent attacks the skin, eyes, lungs, and gastrointestinal tract. Internal organs, mainly blood-generating organs, may also be injured, as a result of mustard agent being taken up through the skin or lungs and transported into the body.

FREQUENTLY ASKED QUESTIONS (FAQ)

Well constructed FAQ sites provide a good front line defense for answering common questions. Provided here are some good examples of FAQ sites on bioterrorism.

Center for Infectious Disease Research & Policy
<http://www1.umn.edu/cidrap/content/bioprep/faqs/faqs-consumer.html>

This site covers various questions on: infectious diseases, likely ways that bioterrorism attacks occur, antibiotics, vaccines, anthrax, water supply, gas masks, food, family safety, etc. This site provides good current information, is easy to read, and covers basic questions. Also, "medical fact sheets" on diseases of bioterrorism provide a good background on specific diseases and can also be found at this site.

Bioterrorism Preparedness
<http://www.hs.state.az.us/phs/edc/edrp/es/btfaq.htm>

This site provides practical, easy-to-read advice on such questions as: What general precautions should the public take regarding the threat of bioterrorism? Are vaccinations recommended in case of a bioterrorism attack? What is the health department doing to protect the public from bioterrorism? Are vaccines for smallpox and anthrax available? This site is from the Arizona Department of Health, and is a good example of a state department information site.

Bioterrorism Concerns after September 11 (Center for Civilian Biodefense Studies)
<http://www.hopkins-biodefense.org/faq.html>

The Johns Hopkins Center compiled this FAQ based on calls they received after September 11. It includes FAQs on coping, gas masks, antibiotics, smallpox, and protecting family members.

Center for the Study of Bioterrorism and Emerging Infections–St. Louis University School of Public Health
<http://www.slu.edu/colleges/sph/bioterrorism/key_ref.htm>

The mission of the Center is to provide public health and health care facilities with the tools needed for preparedness, response, recovery, and mitigation of intentional or naturally occurring outbreaks (see Figure 1). This site provides good information on planning for government agencies and hospitals.

CHILDREN/FAMILY ORIENTED INFORMATION

Resources that are specifically geared toward family and children provide good information to allay fears. Children can be susceptible to the same fears as adults, but may not have the communication skills to express their fears in a healthy way. These sites provide resources and advice on ways to communicate with children on the threat of bioterrorism.

For Children–American Academy of Pediatrics
<http://www.aap.org/advocacy/releases/anthraxqa.htm>

"It is important to allow children to express their fears and concerns and to communicate to them that they are safe." This site focuses specifically on Anthrax and bioterrorism; however, the advice that is given

FIGURE 1. Center for the Study of Bioterrorism and Emerging Infections (St. Louis School of Public Health)

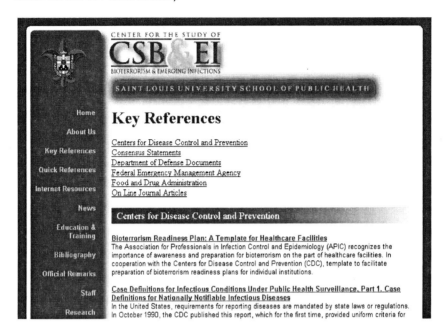

can be applied to talking to children about many other possible threats. A search capability is provided.

For Teenagers–Smallpox, Anthrax and Terrorism
<http://kidshealth.org/misc_pages/T_squarebanner.html>

This site provides information for teenagers written in a language they can understand and relate to. Hints are provided on ways to "Share your feelings" and "Give yourself a reality check." This is good advice for anyone. A search capability is provided.

American Academy of Pediatrics Family Readiness Kit
<http://www.aap.org/family/frk/frkit.htm>

This kit is for parents to use at home to help prepare for most kinds of disasters. In most families, mothers are likely to handle this responsibility. However, other family members often help too–fathers, grandparents, and even children. The information on this site was compiled after surveying 250 families. Although the site deals mostly with general emergencies such as floods and hurricanes it does provide ways to handle the family situation in other emergencies. A search capability is provided.

FOOD SAFETY

The food supply could possibly be a vector used by terrorists. These resources provide information on how the public can be more aware of the potential threat and be able to better protect itself.

Division of Bacterial and Mycotic Diseases–Botulism FAQs
<http://www.cdc.gov/ncidod/dbmd/diseaseinfo/botulism_g.htm>

This site provides information on diagnosis, treatment, and prevention of food-born botulism (see Figure 2). Botulism can be prevented fairly easily and this site provides some practical advice on ways to avoid it. A search capability is provided.

Frequently Asked Consumer Questions About Food Safety and Terrorism
<http://www.cfsan.fda.gov/~dms/fsterrqa.html>

The USDA's Center for Food Safety and Applied Nutrition has created this site to provide information on the measures being taken to protect the food supply and addresses such questions as "Should consumers take antibiotics for protection against contaminated food?"

GENERAL RESOURCES

These are important sites for information that does not necessarily fit into other categories.

Public Health Emergency Preparedness and Response
<http://www.bt.cdc.gov/>

This very comprehensive site from the Center for Disease Control has good up-to-date information and provides links to CDC alerts and

FIGURE 2. Division of Bacterial and Mycotic Diseases–FAQs

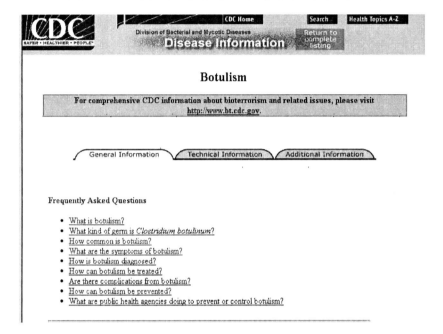

fact sheets. It also contains information on vaccines and planning for emergencies. A search capability is provided.

Center for Civilian Biodefense Strategies (Johns Hopkins University)
<http://www.hopkins-biodefense.org/>

The site contains information for both the general public and public health officials. The links to the *JAMA* consensus statements provide information on the history, prevention, epidemiology, therapy, research, and other in-depth information on a number of key potential agents.

Health Aspects of Biological and Chemical Weapons (OMNI)
<http://omni.ac.uk/whatsnew/detail/3015504.html>

OMNI is the "UK's Gateway to High Quality Internet Resources on Health and Medicine" (see Figure 3). This site includes some interesting links, and is the United Kingdom equivalent of the Johns Hopkins

FIGURE 3. Health Aspects of Biological and Chemical Weapons (OMNI)

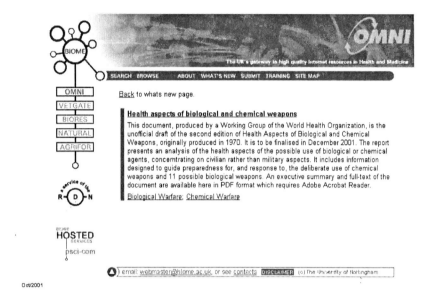

site. Much of this information is aimed at public health professionals rather than consumers. A search capability is provided.

Chemical Weapons and Chemical Weapons Protection from OPCW (Organization for the Prohibition of Chemical Weapons) <http://www.opcw.nl/chemhaz/chemhome.htm>

This site has links to information on different agents including–Nerve Agents, Mustard Agents, Hydrogen Cyanide, Tear Gases, Arsines, Psychotomimetic Agents, Toxins, and potential chemical weapon agents. In addition there is information on prevention, both military and civilian, and information on chemical accidents. This is a good source for definitions and prevention discussions.

GOVERNMENT SOURCES

Many government agencies provide information on bioterrorism, prevention, detection, and response as well as general information to allay fears and to have the public and professionals be prepared. This is by no means an exhaustive list; however, listed here are some of these government resources that can be found on the Internet.

Public Health Emergency Preparedness and Response (Center for Disease Control)
<http://www.bt.cdc.gov/>

This CDC site is very comprehensive, and one that kept appearing in various searches. Fact sheets and FAQs are provided, along with statistical and educational resources. A search capability is provided.

Office of Disease Prevention and Health Promotion
<http://odphp.osophs.dhhs.gov/>

The Office of Disease Prevention and Health Promotion works with other government agencies to strengthen the disease prevention and health promotion priorities. This site includes announcements, online publications, and other links. There is information for children, adults, consumers, and professionals, and some information is included in Spanish as well as English.

Center for the Study of Bioterrorism and Emerging Infections (St. Louis University School of Public Health)
<http://www.slu.edu/colleges/sph/bioterrorism/Internet/government.htm>

This site provides a very comprehensive list of links to government agencies. The agencies are categorized by broad topics that include: Public Health, Environment, Emergency Management, Crisis management, and the Department of Defense.

MEDICALLY RELATED SOURCES

These sites are produced by the medical community to provide information to professionals. However, some of the information included is in consumer health format.

Biological and Chemical Weapons (NLM and NIH)
<http://www.nlm.nih.gov/medlineplus/biologicalandchemicalweapons.html>

This site is very comprehensive with numerous links to more in depth information. It is well organized by the following categories–Latest

News, General Overviews, Alternative Therapy, Coping, Prevention and Screening, Research, Specific Conditions and Aspects, Directories, Organizations, Children, Teenagers, Spanish Speaking. A search capability is provided.

Medscape Resource Center
<http://www.medscape.com/Medscape/features/ResourceCenter/
BioTerr/public/RC-index-BioTerr.html>

This site is a regularly updated collection of Medscape's key clinical content on the latest findings about bioterrorism. It includes information from recent conferences and other up-to-the-minute resources available on Medscape. Search capability provided.

MENTAL HEALTH INFORMATION

The terror aspects of bioterrorism could be the most devastating, while not being the most obvious. While disease detection and prevention is the focus of much of the media coverage and health community, the mental health aspects of terrorism can be extremely debilitating to many in the population, even those not directly affected. These sites have information on various aspects of mental health and terrorism.

Center for Mental Health Services–Knowledge Exchange
<http://www.mentalhealth.org/publications/allpubs/KEN-01-0095/
default.asp>

This site addresses the mental health aspects of terrorism. "No one who sees a disaster is untouched by it." The various symptoms of stress from terrorism are addressed along with information on both individual and community trauma. A search capability is provided.

Psychology in Daily Life: Coping with Terrorism–APA
<http://helping.apa.org/daily/terrorism.html>

This site from the American Psychological Association outlines the symptoms of trauma from terrorism, including fear and anxiety as well as fear and hatred of foreigners. It provides information and links to resources with good advice on coping mechanisms. A search capability is provided.

CONCLUSION

These are only a few of the many comprehensive resources on bioterrorism available over the Internet. Government, public health departments, hospitals, and a variety of organizations have created Web resources, answering many questions and providing invaluable information for planning and prevention. Most are updated regularly as new information becomes available. Hint: to maximize your Internet search results, in addition to the term bioterrorism, other versions of the term that can be used are: bio terrorism (and terror), bio-terrorism, biological terrorism, and chem-bio terrorism.

Live links to the resources cited here and other sites are available at <http://www.fcii.arizona.edu/dlearn/bio/bioterr.htm>.

Political Violence and Islam:
Definitions and Web Resources

Kate Maragliano

SUMMARY. This article seeks to clarify certain key terms and issues surrounding terrorism in the Middle East and its relationship to the United States. In an effort to do so, some historical background must be provided concerning the dynamics of both political and religious Islam. Included is a list of Internet resources that explore various Islamic terrorist groups in detail. Some Web sites concerning the most recent attacks against the national security of the United States are also provided. *[Article copies available for a fee from The Haworth Document Delivery Service: 1-800-HAWORTH. E-mail address: <getinfo@haworthpressinc.com> Website: <http://www.HaworthPress.com> © 2002 by The Haworth Press, Inc. All rights reserved.]*

KEYWORDS. al-Qaida, al-Qaeda, Islam, Internet, Osama bin Laden, political violence, Taliban, terrorism

INTRODUCTION

Terrorism is the unlawful use of force or violence against persons or property to intimidate or coerce a government, the civilian pop-

---

Kate Maragliano (kmaragliano@hilbert.edu) is Acquisitions Librarian, McGrath Library, Hilbert College, 5200 South Park Avenue, Hamburg, NY 14075.

[Haworth co-indexing entry note]: "Political Violence and Islam: Definitions and Web Resources." Maragliano, Kate. Co-published simultaneously in *Internet Reference Services Quarterly* (The Haworth Information Press, an imprint of The Haworth Press, Inc.) Vol. 6, No. 3/4, 2002, pp. 47-58; and: *Bioterrorism and Political Violence: Web Resources* (ed: M. Sandra Wood) The Haworth Information Press, an imprint of The Haworth Press, Inc., 2002, pp. 47-58. Single or multiple copies of this article are available for a fee from The Haworth Document Delivery Service [1-800-HAWORTH, 9:00 a.m. - 5:00 p.m. (EST). E-mail address: getinfo@haworthpressinc.com].

ulation, or any segment thereof, in furtherance of political or social objectives.[1]

It is impossible to have a singular definition for terrorism, for the term itself reflects an act that can have multiple motives and effects. In addition to the selected definition above, several individuals, institutions, and federal departments have comprised their own meanings of terrorism. Despite the technical variations, some major common themes run throughout, those being coercion, pre-calculated, political motivation, and violence. No matter how it is stated, terrorism as a term brings to mind connotations that are intrinsically negative.

The purpose of this article is to provide a basic background of the emergence of militant Islamic groups in the context of their most recent terrorist acts against the United States. It is also important to make the distinction between Political Islam and Religious Islam, for the dynamics of each are inherently different.

Political Islam, also known as Islamism, emerged in the Middle East at the end of the Cold War when the United States assisted the Islamic resistance against the Soviet occupation of Afghanistan. It was that intervention which lead to the West's increased interest in the environment of the Islamic society. Unknowingly to the United States, it was this strong interest, in combination with Afghanistan's pre-existing crumbling and chaotic political structure that provided a foundation to the Islamic fundamentalist movement in the 1990s. Western-inspired laws and culture have infused most Islamic states partially as a result of U.S. aid during the Soviet occupation in Afghanistan. These secular laws contradict most Islamic beliefs, and the focus of the radical Islamic groups is to restore Muslim laws that are in concordance with the *shari'a*. Any laws outside the framework of the *shari'a* are rejected. In addition, it is their prerogative to eliminate all Western cultural influences, which are regarded as a threat to the Arab-Islamic culture.

Although militant Islamic groups profess a religious framework surrounding their movement to restore the "true" Islamic path, the forceful means they use to express their political ideals has spread much tension throughout the world. How is it, then, that a culture with a peaceful religious vocabulary can commit such acts in the name of religion? Where and how did militant Islamic factions come from?

The emergence of Islam was based upon the idea of total belief in the divine while living on Earth. To maintain that belief, a complex system of laws and principles were followed to create balance and compassion. Those religious practices of Islam lie in the teachings of the Quran (Koran), which is used as a book of spiritual guidance throughout life on Earth. Although balance and order are the main thrusts of Islam, the constant presence of internal warfare has only resulted in political and economic instability. The issues are, more often than not, either political, tribal, or ethnic instead of Islamic. Such unrest has lead to the breakdown of law and order and ultimately, the loss of faith in the administrative and political systems.[2] Consequently, those societies have broken away from the Islamic ideals based on the teachings of the Quran and the life of the Prophet Muhammed. The dissatisfaction with society has increased as they move further away from these ideals and yet, at the same time, the urgency to reconnect with those ideals has become stronger.

Although some fundamentalist groups take a non-violent approach to the restoration of Muslim religious values, other radicals like the *Taliban* commit themselves to violence to attain their goals. These fundamentalists believe that the "right path" can be achieved only by the uses of terror and violence and claim that God has sanctioned *jihad* as a means to resurrect the true Islamic state. Although *jihad* is noted in the Quran as a means to "correct a wrong and command the right" it is emphasized that, initially, all peaceful attempts must be made.

The Taliban regime emerged in the mid-1990s and became a new force in Afghan politics. The regime stormed through the country and took control of its major southern villages and imposed a literal version of Islam that was not at all in accordance with the original ideals of the Islamic faith. The force of the Taliban's control over the Afghan people was extremely harsh and spread throughout most of the country.

The al-Qaida network (also spelled al-Qaeda), created, funded, and led by Osama bin Laden, is comprised of several militant Islamic groups. The Taliban is just one of these groups involved. After the Soviet withdrawal, bin Laden was disgusted with the rampant evidence of Western cultural imperialism that resided, ". . . women disobeying Islamic law in their dress and Westerners flaunting themselves on the streets and drinking alcohol. He later claimed that it was like an American colony."[3] Thus, al Qaida was formed to rid the country of those influences.

CRITERIA FOR WEB SITE SELECTION

The following Web sites were selected to provide a more thorough background regarding terrorism in the Middle East. The focus of this list is to highlight sites devoted to providing information regarding political Islam and the network of terrorist groups that support it. Some sites pertaining to the September 11th attacks and counter terrorist efforts made by the United States are included as well as those with definitions surrounding religious and political Islam. Some key terms are given in Appendix A following this list.

The selection process wasn't an easy one since there are a myriad of sites pertinent to the subjects of terrorism and U.S. national security. Although Internet news sources are updated daily, this author chose to highlight resources created and evaluated by more scholarly sources such as academic institutions, government Web sources, and organizations specifically devoted to terrorist research. By no means should this list be considered exhaustive, for the number of relevant Web sites far exceeds what is provided in this text. The main prerogative of this list is merely to provide the reader with a basis from which to begin research. Images are provided for several main pages.

Despite the vast amount of information on the Internet, there are a number of key print resources that are valuable when researching terrorism. Thus, a list of Indispensable Print Resources appears as Appendix B.

SELECTED SITES OF INTEREST

The World Trade Center Attack: The Official Documents (Columbia university)
<http://www.columbia.edu/cu/lweb/indiv/dsc/wtc.html>

A generous list of several executive branch departments and agencies that have responsibilities in matters concerning terrorism is provided in this site. Links to primary presidential and executive remarks, orders, proclamations, and addresses are listed as well as recent legislation passed into law and bills still in process. Various background documents including airport, army, and homeland security are provided. Patterns of global terrorism, the indictment of Osama bin Laden, and significant terrorist incidents from 1980 to the present are also recorded. International responses to 9/11/01 including statements of concern and support made by NATO, UK, Russia, and the Organization of the Islamic Conferences are included as are documents concerning New York State and New York City and the proposed recovery plan for the World Trade Center.

Columbia Electronic Encyclopedia
<http://www.encyclopedia.com>

Some of the searchable terms in this encyclopedia are Hamas, Muslim Brotherhood, Quran, and Taliban. To the right of the terminology descriptions is a list of articles related to the subject searched. To view an article you must first subscribe to the fee-based service provided by eLibrary and enter your password to access each article.

California State University. Center for the Study
of Hate and Extremism
International Terrorism: Bin Laden's Al-Qaida
and Other Middle Eastern Terrorist Groups
<http://www.hatemonitor.org/international_terrorism.htm>

This site presents descriptions of the al-Qaida terrorist network and other Middle Eastern terrorist groups. The majority of information is taken from the U.S. State Department's "Patterns of Global Terrorism: 2000," in addition to information from Yahudit Barsky of the American Jewish Committee.

University of Pittsburgh School of Law
Jurist: The Legal Education Network; Terrorism Law and Policy
<http://jurist.law.pitt.edu/terrorism.htm>

This site is updated daily with the ability to search the previous two months. It also provides an area to search terrorism laws, reports, hearings, briefings, and papers. In-depth information on terrorism and terrorists, including recent advisories regarding suspicious mail, the possibility of future attacks, is included. A terrorist fact sheet designed by the Federal Emergency Management Agency is provided as well. Several recognized definitions of terrorism are listed in addition to motivations, causes and significant facts, figures, and incidents from around the globe. Also included is some background information on Osama bin Laden and the al-Qaida terrorist network and other FBI most-wanted terrorists. An extensive list of recently adopted anti-terrorism laws in the United States is provided as well as a lengthy list of links to several terrorism research centers throughout the country. A comprehensive bibliography for further research in academic studies of terrorism law and policy is listed in which both print and electronic resources are included.

The Brookings Institution
<http://www.brook.edu/terrorism/>

The Brookings Institution is a private organization concerned with public policy issues of the nation. The President of the United States is the chief administrative officer for creating and coordinating policies, approving publications, and recommending projects. The section titled "America's Response to Terrorism" provides commentary, analysis, and other resources on counterterrorism in the United States.

National Security Archive
<http://www.gwu.edu/~nsarchiv/NSAEBB/sept11/>

This site presents a list of electronic sourcebooks pertaining to the September 11th terrorist attacks. Subjects covered in each volume are listed and updated regularly. For example, Volume I is "Terrorism and U.S. Policy." A unique and useful feature is the option to join the Archives' electronic mailing list to receive an e-mail alert each time new information is added to the site.

Terrorismfiles.org
<http://www.terrorismfiles.org>

Created by Nabou.com, Terrorismfiles.org lists several terrorist organizations from around the world including Middle Eastern groups such as Hammas, al-Qaida, Hizballah, and Mujahedin-e Khalq. Links to comprehensive information on each group including other names, organization biographies, activities, and areas of operation are provided (see Figure 1).

Foreign Affairs
The Terrorist Attacks on America: Background
<http://www.foreignaffairs.org/home/terrorism.asp>

A wealth of previously published articles concerning the recent attacks on America are listed here. Additional essays that outline contemporary terrorism and the resources the United States has to combat future attacks are also included. More importantly, articles that focus on the Middle Eastern and radical Islamic groups are included. In addition, several full-text reviews of print-related books are listed.

FIGURE 1. Terrorismfiles.org

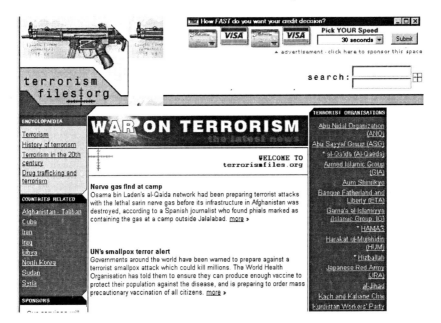

Political Terrorism Database
<http://polisci.home.mindspring.com/ptd>

This site provides several resources on terrorism and political violence. The database explores many definitions of terrorism, group structures, weaponry, tactics, and other Web resources on political terrorism. In addition to providing information on Middle Eastern terrorism, the database includes terrorist information in Latin America, Europe, Asia, and Africa.

Law Library Resource Xchange: LLRX.com
<http://www.llrx.com/features/terrorbiblio.htm>

The Law Library Resource Xchange contains an extensive bibliography on terrorism, bioterrorism, the Middle East, and issues related to September 11th. It also provides links to book reviews on the above mentioned subjects including Islam, Afghanistan, and United States foreign policy. More importantly, it offers a link to a bibliography compiled by the Association of American University Presses for resources specifically pertaining to the September 11th attacks on America.

Terrorism Research Center (TRC)
Site at GeoCities: <http://geocities.com/CapitolHill/2468/trc2.html>
Expanded site: <http://www.terrorism.com>

As an independent institute, the main focus is to provide information on all issues surrounding terrorism research. A network of research specialists from around the globe contribute their expertise from various work environments such as industry, government, and academic institutions. The GeoCities site allows one to search essays, links, several definitions of terrorism, and current events. The expanded site provides a more in-depth look at their resources on terrorism. In addition to a comprehensive list of academic and government links, terrorism analysis, commentaries, and essays are provided. Electronic documents concerned with counterterrorism and profiles of counterterrorist groups and terrorist organizations are included. The TRC is widely recognized by various notable news sources, U.S. Government offices, professional organizations, and publications.

International Center for Terrorism Studies (ICTS)
<http://www.potomacinstitute.org/icts/icts.htm>

Similar to the Terrorism Research Center, the ICTS is an organization independent of any federal or state agency and is structured by the research of experts in the fields of business, government, and academia. As stated on its site, the organization's primary goals are to monitor current and future threats of terrorism, develop counterterrorism strategies, promote communication among the Center's global participants, and sponsor research programs on important issues. Links to government and other organizational Web sites on terrorism are provided as well as current projects and publications.

National Security Institute
<http://www.nsi.org>

The National Security Institute provides information concerning legislation and executive orders on counterterrorism, terrorist profiles, a fact sheet on terrorism, and various other links pertaining to terrorist precautions and commentary. Perhaps the most valuable asset to the site is the CRS Report to Congress that lists, in detail, other Near Eastern terrorist groups and state sponsors.

International Policy Institute for Counter-Terrorism
<http://www.ict.org.il>

Located in Herzlia, Israel, the Institute provides an astounding collection of current articles, documents, and commentary concerning terrorism and, more specifically, Osama bin Laden and his al-Qaida network. A comprehensive list of links to other relevant academic and research centers, public and private organizations, and government sites is provided (see Figure 2).

U.S. Department of State
Terrorist Attacks on the World Trade Center and the Pentagon
<http://usinfo.state.gov/topical/pol/terror/economic.htm>

This site is created and maintained by the Office of International Information Programs of the U.S. Department of State (see Figure 3). Beginning with September 12th, there is an almost daily list of accounts

FIGURE 2. International Policy Institute for Counter-Terrorism

FIGURE 3. U.S. Department of State. Terrorist Attacks on the World Trade Center and the Pentagon

U.S. DEPARTMENT OF STATE
INTERNATIONAL INFORMATION PROGRAMS

International Security | Response to Terrorism

Terrorist Attacks on the World Trade Center and the Pentagon

Economic Issues

• IIP's Economic Security homepage

15 January 2002
Joint Report Says $15,000 Million Needed for Afghanistan
UN Estimates Afghanistan Needs $15,000 Million Aid Over 10 Years

10 January 2002
Treasury's O'Neill to Attend Afghan Aid Conference in Japan
Bush Signs $15,400 Million Foreign Operations Bill
Bush Signs $318 Billion Defense Spending Bill

31 December 2001
U.S. Freezes Assets of Six More Groups Linked to Terrorism

09 January 2002
O'Neill Reports Progress Against Terrorist Financing
Fact Sheet: U.S. Blocks Assets of Two Terrorist-Funding Groups

20 December 2001
Fact Sheet: Bush Blocks Assets of Two More Terrorist Groups
Bush Orders Freeze on Additional Terrorist Assets

19 December 2001
U.S. Trade Deficit Close to Level Before Terrorist Attacks

and updates regarding the nation's response to the September 11th attacks. Statements on the U.S. economy, the tracking and freezing of terrorist financial funding, and new measures taken in aviation security are provided. Links to text regarding the U.S. response to terrorism and international security are also available.

NOTES

1. FBI definition.
2. Akbar S. Ahmed, *Islam Today: A Short Introduction to the Muslim World.* NewYork: I.B Tauris Publishers, 2001.
3. Simon Reeve, *The New Jackals: Ramzi Yousef, Osama bin Laden and the Future of Terrorism.* Boston: Northeastern University Press, 1999.

4. Yonah Alexander and Michael S. Swetnam, *Usama bin Laden's al-Qaida: Profile of a Terrorist Network*. Ardsley, NY: Transnational Publishers, Inc. 2001.

5. Azima A. Nanji, ed., *The Muslim Almanac*. Detroit: Gale Research Inc., 1996.

6. Ibid.

7. Ibid.

8. Ibid.

9. Milton Beardon, "Afghanistan, Graveyard of Empires." *Foreign Affairs*. Nov/Dec 2001: 17-31. *Academic Search Elite*. EBSCOhost. Hilbert College, Hamburg. 31 October 2001.

APPENDIX A

Al-Qaida–Literally means "The Base." Also spelled al-Qaeda. An informal organization created and lead by Osama bin Laden. The network is comprised of extremist Arab-Afghans who spread al-Qaida's ideologies via acts of terrorism. Various terrorist groups and individuals from over fifty countries pledge their support to al-Qaida.[4]

Jihad–Literally means "holy war." More broadly defined as striving to command the right and prevent the wrong through peaceful means such as education and service or war, if deemed necessary. May also be interpreted on a more personal level where one may purify one's self to settle an internal struggle. When referred to war, the Koran specifically describes the conditions of war, peace, treatment of prisoners, and resolution of conflict. The main focus is that the purpose of God's word was to invite and guide people to the "ways of peace."[5]

Koran (Quran)–Muslim holy book revealed to the prophet Mohammad by God through the Angel Gabriel.[6]

Political Islam (i.e., Islamism)–Began in the Middle East during the latter half of the Twentieth Century. Its primary goals are to replace previous "Western-inspired" laws with those that are specifically Islamic; ones that contain the ideologies and structure of the *Shari'a*. Most commonly associated in the Western culture with the term "fundamentalism."[7]

Shari'a–Arabic term referring to traditional Islamic law, literally meaning a pathway to a water hole in the desert. Many Arab contemporaries to the prophet Muhammad resided in the desert and were influenced by the ways of its terrain; water and direction were therefore essential for existence. Laws of Allah that were revealed to his Prophets were referred to as the shari'a.[8]

Taliban–Derived from a Persian word meaning Islamic students or seekers. The regime, under the initial leadership of Mullah Mohammad Omar, was formed in the 1990s, some years after the Soviets left Afghanistan.[9]

APPENDIX B

INDISPENSABLE PRINT SOURCES

1. Ahmed, Akbar S. *Islam Today: A Short Introduction to the Muslim World.* NewYork: I.B Tauris Publishers, 2001.
2. Alexander, Yonah and Michael S. Swetnam. *Usama bin Laden's al-Qaida: Profile of a Terrorist Network.* Ardsley, NY: Transnational Publishers, Inc., 2001.
3. Bergen, Peter L. *Holy War Inc.: Inside the Secret World of Osama bin Laden.* New York: The Free Press, 2001.
4. Fregosi, Paul. *Jihad in the West: Muslim Conquest from the 7th to the 21st Centuries.* Amherst: Prometheus Books, 1998.
5. Khashan, Hilal. "The New World Order and the Tempo of Militant Islam." *British Journal of Middle Eastern Studies* (May 1997): 5-25. Available: Academic Search Elite. EBSCOhost. Hilbert College, Hamburg. Accessed: October 31, 2001.
6. Nanji, Azim A. ed. *The Muslim Almanac.* Detroit, MI: Gale Research, Inc., 1996.
7. Pillar, Paul R. *Terrorism and U.S. Foreign Policy.* Washington, D.C.: Brookings Institution Press, 2001.
8. Reeve, Simon. *The New Jackals: Ramzi Yousef, Osama bin Laden and the Future of Terrorism.* Boston: Northeastern University Press, 1999.

September 11, 2001:
Special Web Sites

Roberta Bronson Fitzpatrick

SUMMARY. The terrorist attacks on the Pentagon and World Trade Center and the United Airlines crash in Pennsylvania on September 11, 2001 shook the world. As part of the outpouring of emotions that were the direct result of the attacks, a number of unique Web sites were developed. Additionally, established sites have included 9-11 information or links. This article presents the author's personal experiences on that day, as well as a brief listing of some interesting and useful Web sites. *[Article copies available for a fee from The Haworth Document Delivery Service: 1-800-HAWORTH. E-mail address: <getinfo@haworthpressinc.com> Website: <http://www.HaworthPress.com> © 2002 by The Haworth Press, Inc. All rights reserved.]*

KEYWORDS. Communications media, disasters, Internet, New York City, Pennsylvania, terrorism, Virginia

INTRODUCTION

It seemed like such an ordinary day at the time. I was attending a meeting at the NYU Health Center with library colleagues Richard

Roberta Bronson Fitzpatrick (fitzparb@umdnj.edu) is Associate Director, George F. Smith Library of the Health Sciences, University of Medicine and Dentistry of New Jersey.

The author wishes to acknowledge Peggy Dreker and Nicole A. Cooke, Information and Education Librarians at the Smith Library, for their valuable contributions of noteworthy Web sites.

[Haworth co-indexing entry note]: "September 11, 2001: Special Web Sites." Fitzpatrick, Roberta Bronson. Co-published simultaneously in *Internet Reference Services Quarterly* (The Haworth Information Press, an imprint of The Haworth Press, Inc.) Vol. 6, No. 3/4, 2002, pp. 59-72; and: *Bioterrorism and Political Violence: Web Resources* (ed: M. Sandra Wood) The Haworth Information Press, an imprint of The Haworth Press, Inc., 2002, pp. 59-72. Single or multiple copies of this article are available for a fee from The Haworth Document Delivery Service [1-800-HAWORTH, 9:00 a.m. - 5:00 p.m. (EST). E-mail address: getinfo@haworthpressinc.com].

Faraino, Gail Hendler, and Colleen Cuddy, a planning session for the upcoming fall training program. The Health Center is located near the NYU campus at Washington Square in Greenwich Village <http://www.nyu.edu/pages/health/> and serves as a source of primary and urgent care, as well as other specialized medical services, for the NYU population. Shortly after the start of the meeting, Dr. Carlo Ciotola from the NYU Health Center received a phone call, informing him that a plane had crashed into the World Trade Center (WTC). Dr. Ciotola connected to the CNN Web site to see if there was any news about the crash. It was difficult to continue the meeting, and there was some discussion about the possibility of assisting victims at the Health Center, given its proximity to the downtown area.

We left our meeting at about the time that the second plane hit the WTC. People were milling around in the streets and there was smoke in the once clear blue sky. Subways had stopped running. We were all wondering how to get back uptown to the NYU Medical Center, which is located about 2.5 miles northeast of the crash site. Finally, a cab stopped in the intersection and we were able to climb in. The driver had come from the area nearer the crashes and he was trembling and crying quietly. He said, "I'll take you anywhere—just not back downtown." We listened to the radio on the way back to the NYU Medical Center. There seemed to be an eerie quiet, broken only by sirens. As we cut across the broad avenues on side streets, we waited while emergency vehicles, fire trucks and engines, police cars, zoomed past us, lights flashing and sirens blaring. At the time, none of us realized that what we were seeing was probably the last response to a call or "last alarm" that many of those police and firefighters would make.

Back at the Medical Center, people were milling about in confusion. Someone had managed to get CNN on the projection screen in one of the lecture halls, and people watched the images in horror as the Towers collapsed, one after the other. The Student Cafeteria was emptied, to serve as a triage center for victims who never arrived. Medical students were sent back and forth to Bellevue Hospital. Every trauma book in the Library's collection was checked out and taken over to Bellevue's Emergency Room. Library computers were always in use, students, faculty, and staff searching for the latest information about what had happened or sending e-mails. I went out to lunch with a colleague. We sat at a small table in a local restaurant. Typically, New Yorkers seated at close tables pretend that they are *not* really dining elbow to elbow with strangers. That day, we all sat and looked at grainy images on a black and white portable television, its rabbit ear antennae augmented with aluminum foil, talking easily and crying with strangers. Afterward, we strolled around Second Avenue, walking in the broad street with ease, as there was absolutely no traffic.

Xiomara Cruz, Library Manager at the NYU Downtown Hospital, called to say that she had been asked to work in a triage center set up in the hospital's cafeteria. There, she took patient information and contacted relatives. Xi sent a digital photo taken from the Library's windows. What was once a view of the World Trade Center was obliterated in a cloud of dust. Xi noted that most of the patients at the Downtown Hospital were pedestrians from the area who had been injured by falling debris or by particulate matter in the air.

In the days that followed, it was absolutely not business as usual. FEMA took over NYU's Ehrman Medical Library <http://library.med. nyu.edu> and victims' relatives came to file reports and to turn over DNA samples. Library service desks were deluged with calls, as the phone numbers were published on various Web sites as being "the" place to call for information about missing persons. There were also calls to the Library about bioterrorism threats, such as anthrax in the subways. It was difficult to walk or drive in the area, as the National Guard and police departments from Long Island set up security checkpoints. There were tents erected in the streets near Bellevue Hospital. Bus and subway service did not appear to follow any regular schedule.

That was my last week of work in Manhattan. It was an effort to provide order in the midst of chaos. I spent part of my last day at NYU huddled in the rain underneath an elevated section of the FDR Drive. We were all sent from the Medical Center, due to a bomb threat in the Dental Clinic.

The events of September 11, 2001 affected everyone in a deeply personal way. You didn't need to be in Manhattan to feel involved. Whether you lost a friend or family member, worked in the area, or watched events unfold on television, the senseless killings that took place on that day are a shared loss.

A great number of Web sites have emerged in the very emotional aftermath of September 11, 2001. This article will present samples of some of the best or most significant sites. In general, the first rule of thumb was to select a site based on the reputation of the author, such as the American Library Association (ALA) or FEMA. If the sites presented information for victim's families, in terms of death benefits, crisis counseling, etc., an attempt was made to locate new pages on existing, reputable sites, such as those from state and local governments or federal agencies. Web sites devoted to the victims were selected based upon either their professional affiliations with the victims, such as special police or fire department pages or the Department of Defense. In the case of victims who were on board the various airlines, there seemed to be nothing noting the loss on the Web pages of either American or United Airlines, so Web sites were chosen that seemed to present the information in a very factual way and that cited the source of their information, e.g., Associated Press. Images of several sites are made available.

THE VICTIMS

Web sites honoring the victims of September 11 are available on the Internet. Some of the best are listed here.

FDNY (Fire Department of New York)
<http://www.ci.nyc.ny.us/html/fdny/html/memorial/index.html>

This site lists the members of the Fire Department "who have made the ultimate sacrifice." It is organized by rank, so users can click on the rank insignia and view an alphabetic list of names, with hotlinks to photos and other information (see Figure 1).

NYPD (New York Police Department)
<http://www.nyc.gov/html/nypd/html/memorial_01.html>

This site contains names and photos of police department personnel lost in the World Trade Center Attack (see Figure 2).

Port Authority of NY & NJ Police
<http://www.nytears.com/port_authority_police_officers_l.htm>

This page contains names and photos of officers lost from the agency responsible for patrolling the port and crossings of the metropolitan New York/New Jersey area, including bridges and tunnels.

United Airlines Flight 93 Memorial
<http://www.flight93.org/heroes_list.html>

This memorial site lists victims of the crash in Western Pennsylvania. Photos are provided for many individuals, as well as brief obituaries and related articles.

FIGURE 1. Fire Department of New York Memorial

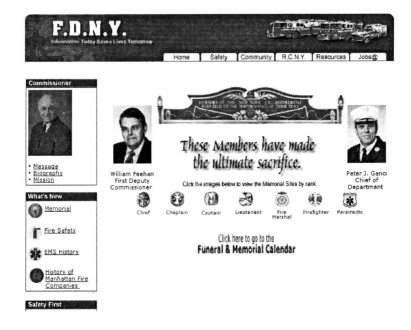

FIGURE 2. New York Police Department Memorial

Rescue 3 FDNY
<http://www.fdnyrescue3.com/wtcmemorial.htm>

A page dedicated to Rescue 3 FDNY. This site is particularly heartbreaking because the photos of the men are not posed, I.D. card-type pictures, but candid action shots taken on "jobs" or at the firehouse. Biographical sketches tell personal details about the firefighters, and the pictures capture a love of job and the camaraderie of the fire service.

Victim Remembrance Site
<http://attacked911tripod.com/>

This is an extremely moving site with a great mix of audio, video, and photographs. Users should note that at times this site is taken down due to "excessive bandwidth consumption."

World Trade Center and Pentagon Memorial
<http://www.worldtradecentermemorial.com/>

This site provides links to individual memorial pages, as well as to news sources, music and poetry, and information resources.

Flight 11 Memorial
<http://www.flight-11.com/>

Names and photos of passengers on American Airlines Flight 11 are presented.

Flight 77
<http://www.rememberalways.com/wtc/victims_aa77.htm>

This site provides names and brief biographical sketches of passengers and crew of American Airlines Flight 77 that crashed into the Pentagon.

Flight 175
<http://www.rememberalways.com/wtc/victims_ua175.htm>

Names and brief biographical sketches of passengers and crew of American Airlines Flight 175 that crashed into the South Tower of the World Trade Center are given at this site.

Flight 93
<http://www.rememberalways.com/wtc/victims_ua93.htm>

This site gives names and brief biographical sketches of passengers and crew of United Airlines Flight 93 that crashed near Shanksville, PA.

Flight 11
<http://www.rememberalways.com/wtc/victims_aa11.htm>

Names and brief biographical sketches of passengers and crew of American Airlines Flight 11 that crashed into the North Tower of the World Trade Center are provided.

Pentagon Victims
<http://www.rememberalways.com/wtc/victims_pentagon.htm>

This site provides a record of names and brief information about service members, employees, and contract workers who died in the attack on the Pentagon, as provided by the Department of Defense.

World Trade Center Victims
<http://www.rememberalways.com/wtc/victims_wtc.htm>

A listing of all World Trade Center Victims and their status, e.g., missing, confirmed dead, etc., is given at this site.

NEWS AND INFORMATION

Following are some general information Web sites about September 11.

Research & Reference Resources Events of Sept 11, 2001
<http://www.freepint.com/gary/91101.html>

Complied by Gary Price, Library and Information Consultant, this is a great site with everything from country maps, congressional testimony, and information on FEMA to the FBI and many fast facts links. It is divided into a number of sections: "New" information section; full-text materials from government sources (U.S. and foreign); full-text articles; Ready Reference/Fast Facts; texts of speeches; streaming audio/video; plus a new Anthrax & Bioterrorism webliography.

The Television Archives
<http://tvnews3.televisionarchive.org/tvarchive/html/index.html>

This site has news coverage of the events of September 11 from around the world.

September 11th Archive
<http://september11.archive.org/>

This collection of archived documents was commissioned by the Library of Congress in order to preserve digital materials covering the events of September 11, 2001. This is a library of Web content from around the globe (see Figure 3).

Associate of American University Presses
<http://aaupnet.org/news/spotlight.html>

"Books for Understanding" devotes a page of resources that are helpful in understanding the events of September 11, 2001.

GOVERNMENT SOURCES

FirstGov–The Official US Government Web Site
<http://www.firstgov.gov/featured/usgresponse.html>

This site contains a wealth of information and links for Victims Benefits and Assistance, including "Protecting Yourself–Mail Handling Tips," "How to help your Country," (becoming an Air Marshall and joining the service), FBI information, Labor information, and travel tips.

Federal Emergency Management Agency (FEMA)
<http://www.fema.gov/nwz01/nwz01_117a.htm>

The FEMA site contains a handy table with victim benefit and assistance contacts. Information is also available in Spanish.

America Responds–News from The White House
<http://www.whitehouse.gov/response>

The White House site contains various Presidential actions and White House News.

FIGURE 3. September 11th Archive

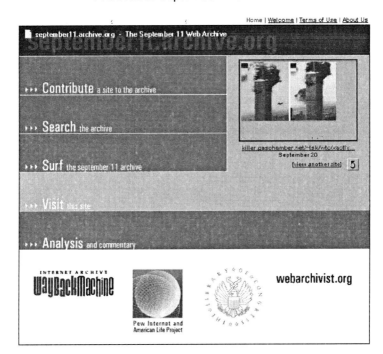

NYC Emergency Information
<http://www.nyc.gov/html/em/home.html>

Information from New York City ("always open") on various services available to victims/families can be found at this site. It also contains federal air quality reports for NYC and public health information.

Hope and Remembrance
<http://www.ojp.usdoj.gov/ovc/vfa/questions/questions_faq.html>

This site was produced by the Office for Victims of Crime–Victims and Family Assistance, U.S. Department of Justice.

U.S. Centers for Disease Control
<http://www.cdc.gov>

The CDC site is updated daily with information on the World Trade Center and bioterrorism.

State of NJ Home Page
<http://www.state.nj.us/>

The state of New Jersey provides great general information for NJ Family Assistance Center and Domestic Preparedness Information. Within this site, the page at <http://www.state.nj.us/wtc/index.html> gives links and Telephone Numbers for all agencies and organizations that families of World Trade Center victims may need including State Police, NJ Department of Banking, U.S. Airline information, and Red Cross contact information.

New Jersey State Police Listing of Missing People
<http://www.njsp.org/wtc_missing.htm>

This is a list of New Jersey residents missing in the World Trade Center attack.

New Jersey Office of Emergency Management
<http://www.state.nj.us/njoem/worldtrade.html>

This is a great site filled with referral information such as phone numbers, recovery information, and counseling services.

State of New York
<http://www.state.ny.us/>

Check out the New York State Web site for helpful information, such as emergency contact phone numbers and press releases.

U.S. Department of Justice
<http://www.usdoj.gov/victimcompensation/index.html>

September 11th Victim Compensation Funds information can be found here.

American Red Cross
<http://www.redcross.org/index_stories.html>

This Web site contains many stories and photo exhibits. Learn how Velveeta and the Red Cross worked together!

JUST FOR KIDS

Here are several fine efforts at collecting resources to help explain the events of September 11 to children.

Teacher Web Site for Kids
<http://teacher.scholastic.com/newszone/specialreports/challenge/index.htm>

This is a Web site for teachers to work with kids in the classroom, in order to help understand the events of September 11th.

Resources for Children and Their Parents and Educators: Dealing with the American Tragedy of September 11, 2001
<http://www.ala.org/alsc/dealing_with_tragedy_web.html>

This is a collection of handy Web sites by the American Library Association (ALA). The list is also available in PDF format.

Resources for Dealing with Loss and Grief (Yale University)
<http://www.yale.edu/21c/resource/resources_for_dealing_with_loss_.htm>

This site contains resources for helping parents discuss September 11th events with their children.

Resources for Coping with the Events of September 11th (Bank Street College Library)
<http://streetcat.bnkst.edu/html/resources.html>

Lesson Plans and bibliography for use in classrooms are included here.

U.S. Department of Education
<http://www.ed.gov/inits/september11/>

This site was designed to help kids understand 9-11-01.

HEALTH RELATED RESOURCES

NJ Hospital Association–NJ Hospitals Respond to Trade Center Disaster
<http://www.njha.com/njresponse>

Contains information about the role played by various New Jersey hospitals on September 11th and of the resources that they continue to provide in the aftermath of the tragedy.

Medscape
<http://www.medscape.com/medscape/features/ResourceCenter/DisasterTrauma/public/RC-index-DisasterTrauma.html>

Medscape's editors have put together this collection of news, notices, articles, and related links to provide health care professionals with the latest information and resources related to caring for those affected by the September 11th terrorist attacks on New York City and Washington, DC.

RESOURCES COMPILED BY LIBRARIES

The Librarians' Index to the Internet
<http://www.lii.org/search>

This site is perhaps one of the most reputable search engines available–please enter "September 11, 2001" (with quotes) as a subject search.

New York State Library–September 11: World Trade Center Information
<http://www.nysl.nysed.gov/library/ann/emerinfo.htm>

A compilation of September 11th information from the New York State Library, this page provides selected links to government sites (both state and federal), disaster recovery resources, and resources for research and background information.

Queens Borough Public Library
<http://www.queenslibrary.org/WTC_News_Sites.asp>

A variety of information (foreign languages included) compiled by the Queens Public Library is contained in this site.

ALA Responds to National Crisis
<http://www.ala.org/pio/crisis/index.html>

This information is provided by the American Library Association.

Kansas City Public Library: September 11, 2001 and the Aftermath
<http://www.kclibrary.org/ref/wtc.htm>

This site includes a variety of interesting news sources, including those not found in the mainstream press, plus a list of "ways you can help" and links to geopolitical Web sites.

Tempe Public Library
<http://www.tempe.gov/library/netsites/11sept01.htm>

Background information and news articles about the World Trade Center and Pentagon attacks are available here.

FINAL THOUGHTS

This brief collection of Web resources really just scratches the surface of what is available and devoted to the topic of September 11, 2001. The resources as presented were available at the time of this writing, November-December 2001, and may change by the time of publication. It is expected that other important or relevant sites will continue to pop up on the Internet.

As a resident of the New York metropolitan area, I still miss the Towers. I look for them as I drive down the New Jersey Turnpike every morning on my way to work. I've also taken to surfing the Net for photos of the Trade Center as it used to be. Two of my favorites are:

Great Buildings.com
<http://www.greatbuildings.com/buildings/World_Trade_Center.
html>

Browse this site for some comforting photos of the twin towers.

World Trade Center Photos
<http://www.worldtradecenterphotos.com/>

See the "before" series for some nice views of the Twin Towers.

Surviving the Attack:
Web Resources on the Emotional Impact
of Terrorism

Patricia E. Gallagher
Marie Tomlinson Ascher

SUMMARY. The recent terrorist attacks have impacted, in one way or another, everyone. For some, the psychological reactions have been debilitating. For the many agencies and organizations whose mission involves helping those with emotional problems, the World Wide Web has provided a venue to communicate help information. The Web also permits those, already distraught, with a means of privately surveying the information, and a means of finding help in the privacy of their own home. The resources discussed here represent an overview of reliable information available for those seeking help. *[Article copies available for a fee from The Haworth Document Delivery Service: 1-800-HAWORTH. E-mail address: <getinfo@haworthpressinc.com> Website: <http://www.HaworthPress. com> © 2002 by The Haworth Press, Inc. All rights reserved.]*

KEYWORDS. Terrorism, posttraumatic stress disorder, disasters, Internet

Patricia E. Gallagher (pgallagher@nyam.org) is Special Projects Coordinator, The New York Academy of Medicine Library, 1216 Fifth Avenue, New York, NY 10029. Marie Tomlinson Ascher is Head, Reference and Information Services, Medical Sciences Library, New York Medical College, Valhalla, NY 10595.

[Haworth co-indexing entry note]: "Surviving the Attack: Web Resources on the Emotional Impact of Terrorism." Gallagher, Patricia E., and Marie Tomlinson Ascher. Co-published simultaneously in *Internet Reference Services Quarterly* (The Haworth Information Press, an imprint of The Haworth Press, Inc.) Vol. 6, No. 3/4, 2002, pp. 73-85; and: *Bioterrorism and Political Violence: Web Resources* (ed: M. Sandra Wood) The Haworth Information Press, an imprint of The Haworth Press, Inc., 2002, pp. 73-85. Single or multiple copies of this article are available for a fee from The Haworth Document Delivery Service [1-800-HAWORTH, 9:00 a.m. - 5:00 p.m. (EST). E-mail address: getinfo@haworthpressinc.com].

73

INTRODUCTION

Disasters leave scars. They kill people and level buildings. They scar those that survive as well, leaving them without homes, without jobs, without loved ones, and with visions of horrors that remain in nightmares for years. Once, a disaster might have affected only those in close geographic proximity to the event. However, as we have learned through the years, our world, due to an omnipresent media, has become a smaller place. We can watch, in real time, as events in distant places occur. On September 11, 2001, our world shrank again as we witnessed the destruction brought upon the World Trade Center, the Pentagon, and so many lives. For many, though nowhere near the disaster itself, the scars will cause hurt for some time to come.

For many, faced with a morass of anxieties, fears, and insecurities, the World Wide Web provided resources through which they could find help, information, and just plain companionship. Many Web sites have sprung up in the wake of September 11 to assist those trying to cope with the loss of loved ones, the emotional traumas caused by repeated viewing of these gruesome images, and the reality that our world will never again be quite the same. The following Web sites represent some of the better ones that can help the general public learn more about what they can do to better cope with this tragedy.

OVERVIEWS OF THE EFFECTS OF DISASTERS AND COPING RESPONSES

Many organizations have set up Web sites to assist the public following September 11th. Some, like the National Center for Post Traumatic Stress Disorder, built on a mission and on materials already available on their Web pages. Others assembled new materials specifically to answer the questions that arose from this particular disaster. These represent some of the best.

Disaster Mental Health: Dealing with the Aftereffects of Terrorism from the National Center for Post Traumatic Stress Disorder <http://www.ncptsd.org/terrorism/index.html>

This site consists of a selection of articles specifically geared for the general public and for the health professional, which discuss the many aspects of posttraumatic stress disorder (PTSD). The site includes a page specific to disasters (see Figure 1). Included are articles on at-risk individuals, such as disaster rescue and response workers, children, and war veterans. An article in Spanish discusses self-care and self-help (also available in English) for disaster victims.

Dealing with Traumatic Events–NOAH:
New York Online Access to Health
<http://www.noah-health.org/english/illness/mentalhealth/ptsd.html>
(English)
<http://www.noah-health.org/spanish/illness/mentalhealth/spmental.
html#tragedia> (Spanish)

NOAH links to various organizations that discuss the effects of traumatic events, including terrorism, and ways in which the individual can cope. Web sites are quality-filtered, and organized into specific topics.

FIGURE 1. Disaster Mental Health: Dealing with the Aftereffects of Terrorism (National Center for Post Traumatic Stress Disorder)

Response to Terrorist Acts Against America–National Institute of Mental Health
<http://www.nimh.nih.gov/outline/responseterrorism.cfm>

The National Institute of Mental Health provides a Web site which links to articles that address the various emotional effects of terrorism (see Figure 2). Conditions addressed are posttraumatic stress disorder, anxiety, and depression; substantial booklets are provided for depression and anxiety. Also included is an article (in easy-to-read English and in Spanish), "Post-Traumatic Stress Disorder (PTSD), A Real Illness."

Coping with the Impact of America's Tragedy
<http://www.medem.com/medlb/article_detaillb.cfm?article_ID= ZZZVJYHCWSC&sub_cat=57>

Formed by an affiliation among many US medical societies, including the American Psychiatric Association and the American Medical Association, this Web site links to five articles which specifically address the emotional response to terrorism and disasters:

- "Coping with a National Tragedy"
- "Communicating with Children About Disasters"
- "Helping Children Cope with Violence"
- "Posttraumatic Stress Disorder"
- "Let's Talk Facts About Posttraumatic Stress Disorder."

Center for Mental Health Services
Disaster Mental Health
<http://www.mentalhealth.org/cmhs/EmergencyServices/>

The following two pages are from this Web site:

Mental Health Aspects of Terrorism
<http://www.mentalhealth.org/publications/allpubs/ KEN-01-0095/default.asp>

Strong emotional reactions to disasters are normal. This concisely worded document outlines some of the usual reactions to disaster, ways in which to speak to another's concerns about their reactions, and the symptoms which may require professional intervention. The document also includes an 800 number that can be called for referral to local mental health counselors.

FIGURE 2. Response to Terrorist Acts Against America (National Institute of Mental Health)

NIMH
National Institute
of Mental Health

Welcome
News & Events
Clinical Trials
Funding
  Opportunities
For the Public
For Practitioners
For Researchers
Intramural Research
Publications
  Order Form
Para Ordenar
  Publicaciones
CRISP
PubMed
Medline Plus
MH Cornerstone
Health Information
Healthfinder

RESPONSE TO TERRORIST ACTS AGAINST AMERICA

POST-TRAUMATIC STRESS DISORDER

• **Helping Children and Adolescents Cope with Violence and Disasters**
  Includes a **Resource List**

• **Post-Traumatic Stress Disorder (PTSD), A Real Illness**
  This material may be of special use to those who need information written in easy-to-understand language.

• **Reliving Trauma: Post-Traumatic Stress Disorder**, Science on Our Minds Series
  A one page fact sheet developed for the White House Conference on Mental Health.

• **Facts About Post-Traumatic Stress Disorder**

• **Children and Violence**

INFORMACIÓN EN ESPAÑOL

• **Trastorno de Estrés Postraumático (PTSD), Una Enfermedad Real**

DEPRESSION

• **Depression** - NIMH Information Resources

• **Depression** - Booklet (27 pages)

Tips for Talking About Disasters
<http://www.mentalhealth.org/cmhs/EmergencyServices/after.asp>

The Center for Mental Health Services of the Department of Health and Human Services has compiled a set of help sheets specifically related to coping with disasters. Fact sheets are available to assist teens, older adults, and disaster workers and include:

- *After a Disaster: Self-Care Tips for Dealing with Stress*
- *A Guide for Older Adults*
- *A Guide for First Responders*
- *After a Disaster: A Guide for Parents and Teachers*
- *After a Disaster: What Teens Can Do*
- *Self-care Tips for Dealing with Stress.*

CHILDREN AND TERRORISM

One of the first concerns for many people as the events of September 11 unfolded, was "How am I going to talk to my children about this?"

Children experience diverse reactions and emotions in response to a disaster. Those charged with caring for children need to pay special attention to meet their needs. The following Web sites address these special needs; the sites are aimed at parents, teachers, counselors, and children themselves.

American Academy of Pediatrics
AAP Offers Advice on Communicating with Children
About Disasters
<http://www.aap.org/advocacy/releases/disastercomm.htm>

The AAP offers these succinct pieces of advice which best sum up strategies in helping children cope with disasters:

- It's important to communicate to children that they're safe. Given what they may have seen on television, they need to know that the violence is isolated to certain areas and they will not be harmed. Parents should try to assure children that they've done everything they can to keep their children safe.
- Adolescents in particular can be hard hit by these kinds of events, and parents might want to watch for signs such as: sleep disturbances, fatigue, lack of pleasure in activities enjoyed previously, and initiation of illicit substance abuse.
- Overexposure to the media can be traumatizing. It's unwise to let children or adolescents view footage of traumatic events over and over. Children and adolescents should not watch these events alone.
- Adults need to help children understand the significance of these events. Discussion is critical. It should be stressed that the terrorist acts are ones of desperation and horror–that there are "bad" people out there, and bad people do bad things. But not all people in a particular group are bad. Children should know that lashing out at members of a particular religious or ethnic group will only cause more harm.

The AAP also offers these documents:

- *How Pediatricians Can Respond to the Psychosocial Implications of Disasters* (AAP Policy statement).
- *Psychosocial Issues for Children and Families in Disasters: A Guide for the Primary Care Physician.*

- *The Pediatrician's Role in Disaster Preparedness* (AAP policy statement).
- *Family Readiness Kit–Preparing to Handle Disasters* including information specific to terrorism.

Helping Children and Adolescents Cope with Violence and Disasters
National Institute of Mental Health
<http://www.nimh.nih.gov/publicat/violence.cfm>

This NIMH publication aims to "tell what is known about the impact of violence and disasters on children and adolescents and suggest steps to minimize long-term emotional harm." It discusses what is known about trauma in children and adolescents in general, and describes typical reactions in children and adolescents in different developmental stages. The fact sheet then discusses ways of helping children work through traumatic events, including information for teachers and school administrators, mental health professionals, and family members. Some prolonged reactions may occur as post-traumatic stress disorder (PTSD), and this condition and its treatment are discussed. Furthermore, the publication ends with a resource list of agencies to contact for assistance in helping children and adolescents cope with violent and disastrous events.

Helping Children Understand the Terrorist Attacks
U.S. Department of Education
<http://www.ed.gov/inits/september11/>

The Department of Education has put together a series of documents designed to help children and educators come to terms with the terrorist attacks (see Figure 3). These include:

- Suggestions for Adults: Talking and Thinking with Children About the Terrorist Attacks
- Suggestions for Educators: Meeting the Needs of Students
- A Letter to Elementary School Students from First Lady Laura Bush
- A Letter to Middle and High School Students from First Lady Laura Bush
- President Bush Participates in Launch of Friendship Through Education Consortium
- School Officials Urged to Prevent Harassment of Muslim and Arab-American Students.

FIGURE 3. Helping Children Understand the Terrorist Attacks (U.S. Department of Education)

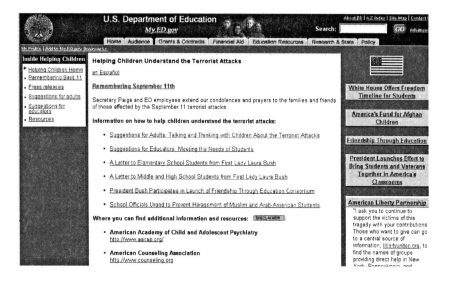

Some of these pages can also be found in Spanish at <http://www. ed.gov/inits/september11/index-es.html>. This site also has a large list of links to other online sources of information about helping children understand the September 11 attacks.

American Academy of Child & Adolescent Psychiatry
Helping Children and Adolescents After a Disaster
<http://www.aacap.org/publications/DisasterResponse/index.htm>

The site includes previously written information in English and Spanish on: "Children and Grief; Helping Children after a Disaster," "Children and the News," and "Posttraumatic Stress Disorder."

Information Written for Children:
Nemours Foundation. KidsHealth
<http://www.kidshealth.org>

The Nemours Foundation offers these articles to help children cope with the terrorist attacks:

- "Dealing with the Terrorist Attacks"
- "Smallpox, Anthrax, and Terrorism"
- "How to Help After the Terrorist Attacks."

FEMA For Kids
<http://www.fema.gov/kids/>

The FEMA For Kids site has several pages designed for children who have been or may be impacted by a disaster. "Disaster Connection: Kids to Kids" provides an outlet for children to express their feelings about disasters and traumatic events. Artwork and letters produced following September 11 and other disasters can be seen. The "Get Ready, Get Set . . ." section includes information on setting a Disaster Plan, putting together a Disaster Supply Kit, and information on "What You Might Feel in a Disaster."

THE MEDIA AND TERRORISM

The effects of television violence have been a topic of discussion for many years now. But when the violence is news, and when those horrific images are aired over and over again for days on end, what effects does this have on you and on your family? These two Web sites discuss the effects of the TV news, and how you can deal with the aftereffects.

Talking with Kids About the News
<http://www.talkingwithkids.org/television/twk-news.html>

The primary focus of this Web document is to discuss the effects of any kind of news violence on children. However, a specific section added after September 11 discusses terrorism on the news and its repercussions for children.

The Effects of the Media Coverage of the Terrorist Attack on the Community
<http://www.ncptsd.org/facts/disasters/fs_media_disaster.html>

Many Web sites discuss the effects of television violence on children. This one addresses the issue in the adult population. In an atmosphere in which the images of destruction were impossible to avoid, this article talks about the impact on all age groups.

BIAS AS A RESPONSE TO TERRORISM

Among the many reactions to the terrorist attacks has been an increase in hate crimes towards Muslim and Islamic Americans. Children are especially susceptible to this kind of reaction, especially when adults are unable to explain their own feelings of anger properly. The following three documents are useful sheets to assist parents and teachers in explaining reactions to terrorism and in preventing inappropriately directed rage from becoming a problem:

When Hurt Leads to Hate: Preventing Your Child's Feelings of Anger from Leading to Actions of Bias and Hate–New York University Child Study Center
<http://www.aboutourkids.org/articles/hate.html>

A National Tragedy: Promoting Tolerance and Peace in Children Tips for Parents and Schools–National Association of School Psychologists
<http://www.nasponline.org/NEAT/tolerance.html>

Talking to Your Child About Hatred and Prejudice–National PTA
<http://www.pta.org/parentinvolvement/helpchild/respectdiff/res ources/talking.asp>

GRIEVING AND BEREAVEMENT

Death is an unfortunate adjunct to any disaster. Resources on grieving are a necessity for people faced with the death of those they love. In some cases, the loss may be in the form of someone declared "missing." Also included is one Web site that discusses the problem of ambiguous loss.

The Compassionate Friends
<http://www.compassionatefriends.org/>

Grieving is not unique to terrorism. The death of any loved one produces trauma, no matter what the circumstance. Compassionate Friends concerns itself primarily with the death of children; however, their brochures on *The Death of an Adult Child, The Death of an Adult Sibling, Parents Who are Now Childless, When a Co-Worker is Grieving the*

Death of a Child, and *When an Employee is Grieving the Death of a Child* are especially useful during this time of grieving.

Coping with Ambiguous Loss–University of Minnesota
<http://ambiguousloss.che.umn.edu/coping.html>

Most of us are used to a "normal" grieving process. A loved one dies, we have a service of some kind, after which the body is ceremonially committed to the earth. However, September 11 presented many families with the problem of mourning when there was no clear evidence of death, save that the person never came home. This document discusses some of the implications facing the grieving families.

Managing Grief After Disaster–National Center
for Posttraumatic Stress Disorder
<http://www.ncptsd.org/facts/disasters/fs_grief_disaster.html>

Though written at a more professional level, this brochure is useful for the descriptions of grieving and traumatic grief, a complication of the grieving process.

How to Deal with Grief–The Center for Mental Health Services
<http://www.mentalhealth.org/publications/allpubs/KEN-01-0104/default.asp>

This fact sheet, which includes a list of support agencies, describes the grieving process, as well as discussing the differences between grief and depression.

Children and Grief–PTA
<http://www.pta.org/parentinvolvement/tragedy/grief.asp>

This detailed article reviews the grieving process in children and discusses the role that adults can play in aiding the child through the grieving process.

Fernside Online
<http://www.fernside.org/>

Based in Cincinnati, Ohio, this agency, which specializes in assisting the bereaved child, has mounted this Web site with resources for both the child and adult. The "Kid's Area" includes an Activities Page, a list of books to read, and e-mail links to which children can send their own questions. The "Grown Up's Area" contains the document "How to Help a Grieving Child," and the "Resources" section contains documents for friends and for educators.

FINDING HELP/HELPING YOURSELF

When someone finds the need for emotional help, where can they go? And how can they understand what exactly is happening to them? The following Web sites discuss the signs and symptoms of stress-related disorders and some ways in which you can help others or help yourself.

Mental Health in Troubled Times–National Mental Health Association
<http://www.nmha.org/reassurance.cfm>

Facts sheets for addressing the concerns of different groups, including children, young adults, college students, adults, older adults, co-workers, and people of faith, are included, along with information on how to cope during the holidays.

Responding to Tragedy–American Counseling Association
<http://www.counseling.org/tragedy/tragedy.htm>

This collection of documents examines ways in which you can help your family, your coworkers, and yourself in acknowledging the emotional effects of disaster. It also includes a list of state crisis hotlines and a fact sheet that explains the job of the professional counselor, as well as ways of finding a counselor.

Handling Anxiety in the Face of the Anthrax Scare
<http://helping.apa.org/daily/anthrax.html>

The idea that bioterrorism is now a threat to everyone has caused mass anxiety in the United States since the attacks of September 11, and the anthrax deaths that followed. These pages are designed to help people better understand the nature of the threat of anthrax and provide suggestions for managing anxiety.

Managing Traumatic Stress: Tips for Recovering from Disasters and Other Traumatic Events
<http://helping.apa.org/daily/traumaticstress.html>

The American Psychological Association has made available two documents to assist the public in dealing with the stress of terrorism. The first examines fears that have resulted from anthrax attacks; the second deals with the impact of September 11 and other disasters. Also available from APA are several other relevant documents (which can be accessed from these two pages).

Red Cross Counseling Materials
<http://www.redcross.org/services/disaster/keepsafe/attack.html>

Included here, in a variety of languages (including Farsi, Tagalog, Russian, and Arabic, among others) are several pamphlets aimed at dealing with the emotional aftereffects of terrorism:

- *How Do I Deal with My Feelings*
- *Helping Young Children Cope with Trauma*
- *When Bad Things Happen*
- *Why Do I Feel Like This?*

Nuclear Terrorism:
A Selection of Internet Resources

Betty Jean Swartz

SUMMARY. In the aftermath of the September 11 catastrophe, the possibility of nuclear terrorism became a real possibility. In this modern world, where nuclear energy and radioactive materials are used in medicine, energy production, the military, and industry, the potential for a terrorist act exists. This article provides a sampling of Internet resources on the history of the nuclear age, the effects of a nuclear accident or a nuclear blast, radiation safety, and nuclear security and terrorism. *[Article copies available for a fee from The Haworth Document Delivery Service: 1-800-HAWORTH. E-mail address: <getinfo@haworthpressinc.com> Website: <http://www.HaworthPress.com> © 2002 by The Haworth Press, Inc. All rights reserved.]*

KEYWORDS. Nuclear terrorism, nuclear accidents, radiation, radioactive materials, Internet

The use of radioactive materials and nuclear energy became common by the end of the 20th century. The development of the atomic bomb and the accidents at Chernobyl and Three Mile Island exhibited the real dangers that this growth presents. In the aftermath of the September 11

Betty Jean Swartz (swartz@umdnj.edu) is Campus Librarian, University of Medicine and Dentistry of New Jersey's UMDNJ and Coriell Research Library, 401 Haddon Avenue, Camden, NJ 08103.

[Haworth co-indexing entry note]: "Nuclear Terrorism: A Selection of Internet Resources." Swartz, Betty Jean. Co-published simultaneously in *Internet Reference Services Quarterly* (The Haworth Information Press, an imprint of The Haworth Press, Inc.) Vol. 6, No. 3/4, 2002, pp. 87-98; and: *Bioterrorism and Political Violence: Web Resources* (ed: M. Sandra Wood) The Haworth Information Press, an imprint of The Haworth Press, Inc., 2002, pp. 87-98. Single or multiple copies of this article are available for a fee from The Haworth Document Delivery Service [1-800-HAWORTH, 9:00 a.m. - 5:00 p.m. (EST). E-mail address: getinfo@haworthpressinc.com].

87

catastrophe, the possibility of nuclear terrorism became a real possibility. In this modern world where nuclear energy and radioactive materials are used in medicine, energy production, the military, and industry, the potential for a terrorist act exists.

This article provides a sampling of Internet resources on the history of the nuclear age, the effects of a nuclear accident or a nuclear blast, radiation safety, and nuclear security and terrorism. Information includes, but is not limited to, documents, databases, fact sheets, search engines, and directories. Sites were chosen on the basis of authority, many of them from U.S. government sources, usefulness and usability, and comprehensiveness.

SEARCHING THE WEB

The Web contains a plethora of information on nuclear terrorism. When selecting sites on nuclear terrorism, as with any other topic, the information should be carefully evaluated.

Search Engines and Directories

The choice of a search engine is often an individual preference. Possible search terms include "nuclear terrorism," "nuclear attack injuries," "health effects of radiation," "nuclear war," or "atomic bomb war." "Chernobyl," "Three Mile Island" or "TMI" may also yield results on the effects of a nuclear disaster. Specific substances such as americium, berkelium, californium, cesium, cobalt, curium, iodine, neptunium, phosphorus, plutonium, radium, strontium, thorium, tritium, or uranium can also be searched.

General search engines, such as Alta Vista <http://www.altavista.com/> and Google <http://www.google.com/>, are favorite tools of many librarians. Using their advanced features will help to increase the number of relevant hits. When searching for U.S. government information, an excellent search tool is First Gov <http://www.firstgov.gov/>.

Directories, unlike most search engines, which use an automated process to locate Web sites, provide selected resources, usually evaluated by an actual person. Several of these, such as Google, Open Directory, and Yahoo! include Nuclear Terrorism as a topic. The path to nuclear terrorism for each of these three directories is listed below.

Google: Society > Issues > Terrorism > Nuclear Terrorism
<http://directory.google.com/Top/Society/Issues/Terrorism/Nuclear_
Terrorism/>

Open Directory: Nuclear Terrorism
<http://dmoz.org/Society/Issues/Terrorism/Nuclear_Terrorism/>

Yahoo! Society and Culture Crime Types of Crime Terrorism
Nuclear Terrorism
<http://dir.yahoo.com/Society_and_Culture/Crime/Types_of_Crime/
Terrorism/Nuclear_Terrorism/>

HISTORY

The specter of nuclear terrorism did not develop in a vacuum. The following sites examine the growth of the nuclear age in the context of the social/cultural, political, economic, and scientific environment. The bombing of Hiroshima and Nagasaki, the Trinity atomic tests from 1945 through 1970, and the human radiation experiments that were performed, often on unwitting subjects beginning in the 1940s, provided vehicles for the study of the effects of a nuclear disaster.

The Atomic Bombings of Hiroshima and Nagasaki
by The Manhattan Engineer District, June 29, 1946
<http://www.yale.edu/lawweb/avalon/abomb/mpmenu.htm>

This document, provided by the Avalon Project at the Yale Law School, examines the effects of the atomic bombs dropped on Hiroshima and Nagasaki. It covers a variety of topics, including the nature of an atomic explosion, types of damage and injuries, and numbers of casualties. Keeping in mind that it was written in 1946, an interesting conclusion was, "Aside from physical injury and damage, the most significant effect of the atomic bombs was the sheer terror which it struck into the peoples of the bombed cities."

Building a Historical Perspective of the Nuclear World
<http://set.lanl.gov/programs/cif/Curriculum/Past/pastmain.htm>

A curriculum from the Los Alamos National Laboratory, this site examines the growth of the nuclear world from prehistoric times through the Cold War and its aftermath.

Human Radiation Experiments (U.S. Department of Energy)
<http://tis.eh.doe.gov/ohre/index.html>

The U.S. Department of Energy maintains a comprehensive re-source, beginning with the 1940s, on human radiation experiments, in-cluding documents, multimedia, oral histories, and more. There is a search engine provided for locating documents in the collection and links to additional DOE and other federal Web sites.

Nuclear Age Timeline (U.S. Department of Energy)
<http://www.em.doe.gov/timeline/>

This history of nuclear energy begins with Wilhelm Roentgen's dis-covery of x-rays in 1895 and culminates with efforts, as of 1993, to clean up the contamination left by the growth of the nuclear age. More than just a timeline, this site provides insight on the social, political, and scientific activities going on at the same time. It is produced by the U.S. Dept. of Energy, Office of Environmental Management.

Trinity Atomic Web Site–Nuclear Weapons: History, Technology, and Consequences in Historic Documents, Photos, and Videos
<http://fas.org/nuke/trinity/index.html>

The Federation of American Scientists provides a multimedia history of atomic testing, with a section on the effects of nuclear weapons.

EFFECTS OF A NUCLEAR DISASTER

The effects of a nuclear disaster or terrorist act could result from a nu-clear blast or from exposure to radioactive material. These sites provide information on the physical, environmental, and health effects of nu-clear material.

Effects of a Nuclear Explosion (Physicians for Social Responsibility)
<http://www.psr.org/Helfand1.htm>

This site from Physicians for Social Responsibility describes the physical and health effects of a nuclear explosion in a major city from ground zero to beyond 16 miles. There is also a section on the effects on medical care.

The Effects of Nuclear Weapons and Nuclear War (Federation of American Scientists)
<http://fas.org/nuke/trinity/nukeffct/>

The Trinity Atomic Web Site from the Federation of American Scientists provides comprehensive information on nuclear explosions. Quicktime videos are included.

The High Energy Weapons Archive: A Guide to Nuclear Weapons (Federation of American Scientists)
<http://www.fas.org/nuke/hew/>

The Federation of American Scientists provides a comprehensive site that includes information about nuclear weapons and their effects. A large number of additional links are provided.

MEDLINEplus: Radiation Exposure
<http://www.nlm.nih.gov/medlineplus/radiationexposure.html>

The already venerable MEDLINEplus provides links to information on radiation exposure, including the latest news on preparations for a possible accident or attack.

MEDLINEplus: Radiation sickness
<http://www.nlm.nih.gov/medlineplus/ency/article/000026.htm>

This article from the MEDLINEplus Medical Encyclopedia is a quick guide to symptoms, precautions, and first aid for radiation sickness. The same information, produced by adam.com, is available on other sites, such as WebMD.

Radiation Effects Research Foundation: A Cooperative Japan-United States Research Organization
<http://www.rerf.or.jp/eigo/experhp/rerfhome.htm>

The RERF (formerly the Atomic Bomb Casualty Commission) was established to study the health effects of the bombings of Hiroshima and Nagasaki. The site includes comprehensive information on radiation effects, scientific data, summaries of reports, and related links.

GOVERNMENT/MILITARY MANUALS

The United States government, primarily the military, provides the full text of several manuals for the assessment, management, and treatment of individuals injured by or exposed to nuclear weapons. Sometimes, as in the first example below, the information is hidden away in an appendix.

Appendix H: Nuclear, Biological, and Chemical Operations (FM 44-43: Bradley Stinger Fighting Vehicle Platoon and Squad Operations, General Dennis J. Reimer Training and Doctrine Digital Library)
<http://155.217.58.58/cgi-bin/atdl.dll/fm/44-43/Apph.htm>

This appendix to a field manual from the U.S. Army Air Defense Artillery School provides practical information on defensive actions to take before, during, and after a nuclear attack and gives first aid tips for blast, thermal radiation, burn, and radiation injuries.

BUMED Instruction 6470.10A–Initial Management of Irradiated or Radioactively Contaminated Personnel
<http://www.vnh.org/BUMEDINST6470.10A/TOC.html>

Substance-specific information is provided in this manual from the Navy's Bureau of Medicine and Surgery and located at the Virtual Naval Hospital site <http://www.vnh.org/>. The entire manual can be downloaded in PDF format.

Chemical/Biological/Radiological Incident Handbook (October 1998)
<http://www.cia.gov/cia/publications/cbr_handbook/cbrbook.htm>

This document from the CIA explains the difference between biological, chemical, and radiological events; includes a table showing what might indicate that a radiological event may have occurred; and supplies a "Glossary of Radiological Terms."

FM 8-10-7: Health Service Support in a Nuclear, Biological, and Chemical Environment (General Dennis J. Reimer Training and Doctrine Digital Library) <http://155.217.58.58/cgi-bin/atdl.dll/fm/8-10-7/toc.htm>

This comprehensive field manual from the U.S. Army Air Defense Artillery School describes the physical, biological, and physiological effects of nuclear weapons; covers types of injuries and management of patients; and includes information on protective shelters and decontamination. There are also sections on the threat of a nuclear incident and planning for services. The references include links to additional manuals.

Medical Management of Radiological Casualties <http://www.afrri.usuhs.mil/www/outreach/pdf/ radiologicalhandbooksp99-2.pdf>

This comprehensive publication from the Armed Forces Radiobiology Research Institute is a comprehensive treatise on handling acute and long-term effects of radiation. There are a very useful section on the psychological effects, lots of tables, and one-page information sheets on individual substances.

Nuclear War Survival Skills <http://www.oism.org/nwss/>

This is a 1987 update of a document originally produced by the Oak Ridge National Laboratory in 1979. This version from the Oregon Institute of Science and Medicine is very easy to navigate and includes a chapter on myths and facts about the dangers of nuclear weapons, practical advice on building and living in a shelter, references, and an index.

DATABASES

HSDB: Hazardous Substances Data Bank <http://toxnet.nlm.nih.gov/cgi-bin/sis/htmlgen?HSDB>

Just enter the substance name into this TOXNET database to retrieve comprehensive information that includes human health effects and emergency medical treatment for radiation exposure.

IRIS: Integrated Risk Information System
<http://toxnet.nlm.nih.gov/cgi-bin/sis/htmlgen?IRIS>

Searching a substance in this TOXNET database retrieves information on carcinogenic and non-carcinogenic effects and a bibliography.

PubMed
<http://www.pubmed.gov/>

MeSH terms for searching PubMed include: "nuclear warfare," "radioactive fallout," "radiation injuries," "accidents, radiation," and "terrorism."

Rapid Response Information System (Federal Emergency Management Agency)
<http://www.rris.fema.gov/>

This FEMA database is searchable by symptoms, chemical or biological agent, or radiological material. Results include symptoms, first aid, and decontamination procedures. There is also information on training courses and a reference library with additional resources.

RADIATION SAFETY AND PREPAREDNESS

Several U.S. government agencies provide information on radiation safety and what to do in an emergency.

Environmental Protection Agency. Radiation Protection Division
<http://www.epa.gov/radiation/>

The EPA's site includes resources for students and teachers, a series of pages on "radiation risks and realities," information on the agency's Radiological Emergency Response Team, a fact sheet on radiation and radiological emergencies, and more (see Figure 1).

International Atomic Energy Agency
<http://www.iaea.org/worldatom/>

The IAEA is concerned with many aspects of atomic energy, including nuclear power plant safety, nuclear waste, arms control, and terrorism.

FIGURE 1

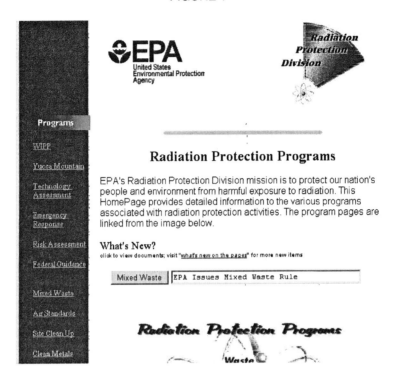

Radiation Protection Programs

EPA's Radiation Protection Division mission is to protect our nation's people and environment from harmful exposure to radiation. This HomePage provides detailed information to the various programs associated with radiation protection activities. The program pages are linked from the image below.

What's New?
click to view documents; visit "what's new on the pages" for more new items

Mixed Waste | EPA Issues Mixed Waste Rule

Ionizing Radiation (Occupational Safety & Health Administration)
<http://www.osha-slc.gov/SLTC/radiationionizing/>

The OSHA site provides annotated links to a number of Web pages and documents categorized under "Recognition," "Evaluation," "Control," "Compliance," "Training," and "Other."

Radiation Protection (U.S. nuclear Regulatory Commission)
<http://www.nrc.gov/what-we-do/radiation/about-radiation.html>

The Nuclear Regulatory Commission Web site houses a wealth of information on radiation safety. There are sections on nuclear reactors, nuclear materials, and radioactive waste, as well as an electronic reading room with even more information.

Radiological Emergency Preparedness Program (Federal Emergency Management Agency)
<http://www.fema.gov/pte/rep/>

This FEMA site is concerned primarily with nuclear power plant safety. Check the FEMA "search" or "site index" links at the top of the page to locate additional FEMA and interagency programs.

NUCLEAR SECURITY AND TERRORISM

Note that some of these sites are posted by environmental or activist organizations. This does not preclude the information from being useful.

International Physicians for the Prevention of Nuclear War
<http://www.ippnw.org/>

Knowing that this is an activist organization's Web site, check particularly the links to "Campaigns," "Events," "Links," and "Publications." This is a good starting point for locating additional Web sites.

Nuclear Control Institute
<http://www.nci.org/>

Although this site is a bit alarmist, it does offer information that won't be found on the government sites and some food for thought. There are links to additional resources.

Nuclear Facts and Figures (Center for Defense Information)
<http://www.cdi.org/nuclear/>

The Center for Defense Information provides a useful site that includes a nuclear weapons database with locations listed worldwide.

Nuclear/Security (Physicians for Social Responsibility)
<http://www.psr.org/securhol.htm>

Physicians for Social Responsibility provide position statements, policy briefs, information on health and environmental effects of nuclear weapons, and more.

Nuclear Terrorism: How to Prevent It (Nuclear Control Institute)
<http://www.nci.org/nci-nt.htm>

The Nuclear Control Institute includes links to several useful sites as well as its own documents.

Unclassified Report to Congress on the Acquisition of Technology Relating to Weapons of Mass Destruction and Advanced Conventional Munitions, 1 July Through 31 December 2000 (Central Intelligence Agency) <http://www.cia.gov/cia/publications/bian/bian_sep_2001.htm>

This is the most recent CIA report, which details for congress the countries acquiring weapons of mass destruction and advanced conventional weapons, and the key countries supplying these weapons. Previous reports can be found on the agency's Publications and Reports page <http://www.cia.gov/cia/publications/pubs.html>.

The War on Terrorism (Central Intelligence Agency) <http://www.cia.gov/terrorism/>

Check this CIA site for press releases, documents, speeches, and links to additional resources (see Figure 2).

FIGURE 2

Central Intelligence Agency   contact us   notices   search   site map   index
Director of Central Intelligence   CIA Home Page

THE WAR ON TERRORISM

Privacy and Security notices   "What are the threats that keep me awake at night?"

About the CIA   "International terrorism, both on its own and in conjunction with narcotics traffickers, international criminals and those seeking
What's New at CIA   weapons of mass destruction. You need go no further than Usama Bin Ladin...."

Employment at the CIA   DCI George J. Tenet, Oscar Iden Lecture,
                          Georgetown University--October 18, 1999

Publications & Reports

The World Factbook
Factbook on Intelligence   ► Public Statements on Terrorism and Usama Bin Laden since July 1997

Speeches & Testimony   ► Public Statements on Potential Terrorist Use of Chemical, Biological, Radiological, and Nuclear (CBRN) Agents since July 1997
Press Releases & Statements

                        ► Terrorism-related Excerpts from Global Trends 2015: A Dialogue About the Future With Nongovernment Experts
Frequently Asked Questions

                        ► Director of Central Intelligence Statements on the Need to Strengthen the Directorate of Operations
Related Links

                        ► Statements to CIA Employees following the September 11th attacks

WWW Sites on Nuclear Terrorism from PRICENet
<http://www.sima.co.at/nucterror.htm>

This family Web site, which is updated regularly, includes a large number of links.

CONCLUSION

This is by no means a comprehensive list of sites relating to nuclear terrorism. The researcher should use the many search engines and directories found on the Web and explore some additional links from the sites in this article.

It Wasn't Raining
When Noah Built the Ark:
Disaster Preparedness for Hospitals
and Medical Librarians Post September 11

SUMMARY. In the wake of the tragic events of September 11, there is an awareness of the critical role of health professionals in disaster response. Hospitals in particular are one important component of the public health system. How prepared are hospitals and medical librarians for a biochemical terrorist event? What does the Internet offer health professionals for readiness for disasters? All hospitals are required by the Joint Commission on Accreditation of Healthcare Organization (JCAHO) to have an emergency management plan, and states' licensure regulations often require a hospital's disaster plan to be comprehensive and filed with a state agency. Thinking the unthinkable, it is prudent for hospitals to strengthen and update their plans for a biochemical terrorist event. This article provides core disaster preparedness information resources updated since September 11 and available on the Internet to assist a hospital. Likewise, medical librarians need to be prepared to respond to the emergency information needs of patrons during such an event and the requests that are often unique, urgent, and sustained. Here, too, a library

Michele Mary Volesko (mvolesko@njha.com) is Director of Library and Corporate Information Services, New Jersey Hospital Association, 760 Alexander Road, P.O. Box 1, Princeton, NJ 08543-0001.

[Haworth co-indexing entry note]: "It Wasn't Raining When Noah Built the Ark: Disaster Preparedness for Hospitals and Medical Librarians Post September 11." Volesko, Michele Mary. Co-published simultaneously in *Internet Reference Services Quarterly* (The Haworth Information Press, an imprint of The Haworth Press, Inc.) Vol. 6, No. 3/4, 2002, pp. 99-131; and: *Bioterrorism and Political Violence: Web Resources* (ed: M. Sandra Wood) The Haworth Information Press, an imprint of The Haworth Press, Inc., 2002, pp. 99-131. Single or multiple copies of this article are available for a fee from The Haworth Document Delivery Service [1-800-HAWORTH, 9:00 a.m. - 5:00 p.m. (EST). E-mail address: getinfo@haworthpressinc.com].

99

"plan" and Internet resources are good starting points. When the disaster strikes, it's too late to start searching for the authoritative resources; they need to be ready and at your fingertips. Using a "Checklist for Medical Librarians: An Algorithm for Disaster Information Preparedness," a medical librarian can assure readiness and offer resources and services that are coordinated and instantaneous. *[Article copies available for a fee from The Haworth Document Delivery Service: 1-800-HAWORTH. E-mail address: <getinfo@haworthpressinc.com> Website: <http://www.HaworthPress. com> © 2002 by The Haworth Press, Inc. All rights reserved.]*

KEYWORDS. Disaster preparedness, disaster response, disasters, hospitals, Internet

INTRODUCTION

Disasters, by their very nature are unpredictable, calamitous, and difficult to conceptualize because they are outside the scope of most experience and thus inherently difficult to anticipate for planning purposes. Posing unique problems, disasters are unlike routine emergencies with their standard procedures and protocols. Complacency and apathy often exist on all levels regarding hospital disaster preparedness programs and though short-lived periods of high profile attention follow a disaster such as September 11, the will and where-with-all to review and improve readiness may be lost if a repeat event is deemed improbable or economic resources unavailable. To further compound the illusion, completion of a written hospital disaster plan is equated to readiness and called the "paper plan" syndrome.[1] What would Noah have asked or changed about the Ark with the hindsight of 40 days of rain at sea?

Perhaps a similar opportunity exists today to ask and answer such questions using Internet resources and ultimately prepare health professionals for new disaster realities. Disaster preparedness is receiving special attention by hospital administrators, health professionals, policy officials, congressmen, and the general public following the terrorist events. This scrutiny offers an improved understanding of the hospital's integral role and resource needs during a disaster. In the wake of the anthrax attacks, hospitals and health professionals faced a disaster of different proportions, from the countless worried well needing medical information to the long lines of potential anthrax infected individuals for Cipro® or nasal swab testing.[2]

Joint Commission on Accreditation of Healthcare Organizations (JCAHO) Disaster Planning Standards

Health care personnel at hospitals, long-term care facilities, and behavioral health facilities should be aware of the environment of care standards that cover disasters. In January 2001, the JCAHO revised EC.1.4, the standard to develop an emergency management plan, to include the need to "address four phases of emergency management activities: mitigation, preparedness, response, and recovery."[3] Standard EC.2.4 requires plan implementation and EC.2.9.1 plan execution with emergency management drills. Based on the events of September 11, JCAHO further states that emergency management and preparedness will be a key survey area for 2002 with a focus on Hazard Vulnerability Assessments (HVAs), involvement of the community in emergency planning and drills, cooperative communication and planning with area health organizations and the health facility's command structure scalability for response to disasters of all magnitudes.[4] What else must hospitals be aware of and comply with to be ready?

State and Federal

States' hospital licensing regulations would require a hospital disaster plan as well as periodic practice drills.[4] In a disaster, state emergency operations plans and the federal response plan may go into effect, and state police, the FBI, and other federal, state, and local emergency management officials play lead or vital roles. Knowing the state and federal process and laws, what entities are involved and their roles, responsibilities, and resources are essential for hospital planning.

Links to learn more about federal organizations and offices with Homeland Security related missions are found on The ANSER Institute for Homeland Security Web page for *Federal Organizations* <http://www.homelandsecurity.org/fedorg.cfm>. State links can be found from each state's official Web site or from a quick list created by FEMA's Global Emergency Management System Web page called *State Emergency Management Agencies (U.S.A.)* <http://www.app1.fema.gov/gems/>. States are not at the same level of terrorism preparedness, and more can be learned from the unique survey results published in October 2001 called *Trends in State Terrorism Preparedness: A Report by the National Emergency Management Association* (NEMA) <http://www.nemaweb.org/Trends_in_Terrorism_Preparedness/Index.htm>. NEMA represents the states' emergency management directors responsible to their governors for disaster preparedness, including acts of terrorism. Integrated efforts, close cooperation, and cross-organizational coordination and communication are needed by all entities involved, especially hospitals. A handy Web page called *Federal Statutes Relevant to Emergency Management* <http://www.state.nj.us/njoem/law_fedlaws.html> is a quick list to federal laws and regulations and the Code of Federal Regulations.

Changing Reality, New Lessons to Learn

Current events that were once unimaginable, coupled by ongoing threats, have changed the dimensions of a hospital's disaster plan from an imaginative exercise to a profound *reality*, one with new-found *urgency*, demanding full attention for a plan's updating and scrutiny. Following September 11, lessons were learned by hospitals on the front lines, by disaster planning officials and others, and new ideas have entered the public consciousness. Health professionals need to access and use this new information to reshape their preparedness for all future events including biological, chemical and nuclear disasters, or warfare such as those involving "dirty" bombs, anthrax, smallpox, plague, brucellosis, botulism, tularemia, Q-fever, viral hemorrhagic fevers, Tabun, Sarin, GF, VX, blistering, blood, or pulmonary chemical agents to name just a few.[6,7]

Sometimes failures in planning are due to not knowing the right questions to ask and understanding why they are so important.[8] Other missteps and miscalculations with the bioterror attacks may have precise important lessons for hospitals, too early to glean.[9] There are authoritative resources on the Internet that can assist in updating disaster planning, some evolving even as this is being published. Importantly, Web resources can assist in redesigning disaster plans to face new and real threats, in understanding the questions to ask, and in remaining up-to-date with the new conclusions being drawn, with the science being rewritten, and with the new lessons terrorism teaches.

To illustrate the changing nature of disaster planning, prophetically, on September 8, Inova Fairfax Hospital in northern Virginia held a mock terrorist attack with a scenario of 160 victims. One month later, Inova Fairfax treated two real victims for anthrax inhalation, postal workers who showed up in the emergency room one day apart. No part of the rehearsal resembled a real attack.[10]

Fact and Fiction: When Worlds Collide

The movie *Dante's Peak* featured a bucolic community nestled in the Cascade Mountains as the town council heard about the potential disaster while experts downplayed the risk, and when the community later learns the true nature of the local threat, it's too late. A volcano erupts and the town's disaster plan remains on the meeting table under debris from earthquakes and volcanic ash. The movie is eerily prescient and a reminder about complacency, the biggest impediment to disaster planning.

Post September 11, truth can be as strange as, or far more real than, fiction. Expecting 5,000 casualties after the collapse of World Trade Center towers one and two, New York and New Jersey hospitals stood "down" from emergency status after 48 hours, when the second wave of massive casualties (sadly) never materialized.[11] Nasal swabs, of no clinical use for anthrax diagnosis, nevertheless became part of the confused public health message.[12] Medical libraries needing Web access found unprecedented Internet traffic and/or inoperable telephone lines, making a paper copy of vital Web documents desired but inaccessible or difficult at best. In the words of Bruce Lawlor, Major General, Joint Task Force Civil Support, "The consequences of WMD [weapons of mass destruction] are so terrible that we cannot afford to think of it as improbable."[13]

DEFINITIONS

Part of disaster preparedness is understanding the unusual nomenclature of disasters and response as well as those of the myriad coordinating agencies at the local, state, and federal level, i.e., the who, what, and where. Even medical experts differ on definitions of mass casualty incidents, and common disaster terminology is important in planning and researching resources. NBC is a good example of the many acronyms used in this field, and is commonly substituted for the phrase "nuclear, biologic chemical."

Potential Injury Creating Event (PICE) Nomenclature

The Potential Injury Creating Event (PICE) nomenclature is taught at emergency planning seminars[14] and identifies common aspects of a disaster and the functional impact of any type of emergency. It is an especially valuable tool in planning for disaster mitigation[15] and considers status of event, resources, geography, and stage. For example, a large-scale earthquake in PICE nomenclature is evolving, paralytic, national, stage III.[16] The PICE system is referenced beginning with the 2001 revisions to the JCAHO standard EC.1.4[17] and additional information on PICE can be found at eMedicine <http://www.emedicine.com/emerg/topic718.htm>.

Disaster Terms, Abbreviations, and Acronyms

Terms, abbreviations, and acronyms such as MCIs, NBC, WMD, mitigation, incident command center, planned improvisation, critical incident stress management, as well as CBIRTs, NPS, CHAIN, USAMRIID are just to name a few. Knowing and using this disaster nomenclature and related terms is key to expanding and targeting database and Web searches in this field. Unfortunately, no one source covers all the terms health professionals will encounter preparing for a disaster, especially ones involving terrorism, due to the multidisciplinary aspects of the topic. The following are Internet reference texts and guides for the topics and fields of disasters, health administration, the military, weapons of mass destruction, September 11 buzz words, and medicine and should cover most needs.

The Department of Defense Dictionary of Military and Associated Terms, a PDF document at <http://www.dtic.mil/doctrine/jel/new_pubs/jp1_02.pdf>, has more than 600 pages of terms and covers those used in bioterrorism and weapons mass destruction. Supplement this with medical sources from the National Library of Medicine's MEDLINEplus Web site including the *adam Health Illustrated Encyclopedia* <http://www.nlm.nih.gov/medlineplus/encyclopedia.html> as well as NLM's links to many online medical dictionaries and glossaries at <http://www.nlm.nih.gov/medlineplus/dictionaries.html>. Other medical associations offer bioterrorism glossaries too numerous to mention and can be found with an advanced search on Google <http://www.google.com> using terms as follows: glossary, nomenclature, dictionary, terms, terminology, and definitions with bioterror as a stem word in the search.

Terrorism and homeland security are important aspects of hospital disaster planning with numerous abbreviations and buzzwords as well as some controversy over definitions.[18] Some general terminology guides are as follows. Steve Buttry's *NewsLab Resources Buzz Words and Catch Phrases: A Glossary for Our Changing World* <http://www.newslab.org/terrorgloss-1.htm#list> was originally created for training purposes and was expanded to cover issues dominating news coverage since September 11, extensively covering terrorism. Two other very extensive glossaries are available. The Monterey Institute's Center for Nonproliferation Studies offers a glossary from its primer *WMD 411* <http://www.nti.org/f_wmd411/gloss.html>. The NBC-MED Web site from the Office of the Surgeon General <http://www.nbc-med.org/others/Default.html> covers nuclear, biologic, and chemical terms.

A specialized authoritative online dictionary for health administration useful for disaster plans is *Slee's Health Care Terms eEdition* <http://www.tringa.com/index.php?submit=HCT>, currently in beta test. Released in October 2001, this 4th edition has more than 6,700 defined terms with links and hierarchical groupings for browsing purposes.

For example, *Slee's* defines a "disaster preparedness plan" as

> A formal plan for coping with a disaster. An accredited hospital is expected to have both an external disaster plan and an internal disaster plan. Often such plans have basic elements relating to any kind of disaster and dealing with such items as emergency communication, alerting of police and fire departments, mobilization of off-duty personnel, and the like. The basic plan also has supplements for various kinds of disasters; for example, a nuclear disaster would call for different procedures than a flood or a tornado. It is expected that the written plan will periodically be tested and modified on the basis of disaster drills.[19]

Comprehending the Incomprehensible: Lessons Learned, Questions to Ask

The JCAHO article, "What the Survey Process Expects of Your Organization," <http://www.jcrinc.com/subscribers/perspectives.asp?durki=1006&site=10&return=1122>, provides countless probing questions hospitals can use for a greater focus on planning. While a hospital is not required to begin a totally new plan in light of recent terrorism, the questions ensure that the plan applies on many different scales, including terrorism.[20] A series of articles called *Lessons Learned* in the December 2001 *Joint Commission Perspectives* <http://www.jcrinc.com/subscribers/perspectives.asp?durki=1010&site=10&return=1122> shares invaluable insights from more than twenty hospitals and organizations responding to September 11. The series includes considerations for managing people and resources effectively, scope of plans, command centers, relationships with other health care organizations and community agencies, self-sufficiency and independence, regional response, backup communications, staging areas, triage, volunteers and resources, decontamination checklists, caring for your own, and mental health needs. The AHA offers a Web area called *Lessons Learned from the Field* <http://www.aha.org/Emergency/Lessons/LessonsIndex.asp> that provides online resources describing integrated community-wide approaches and experience-based reviews from real disasters including Aum Shinrikyo, September 11, Oklahoma City bombing, Houston floods, Florida fires, the 1998 northeastern great ice storm, and Hurricane Floyd, as well as scenario-based exercises including Dark Winter, anthrax, and *Yersinia pestis* aerosol. These frank and real observations offer the new "normal" for the new planning.

Education and Training

Without education to update knowledge and practice skills, effective planning is not possible. Education goes hand in glove with all readiness activities. Some useful Web sites for training opportunities are described here, although readers should also look at all the other Web sites mentioned throughout this article, since most also offer education and training resources as well. The variety of Internet-based educational offerings and resources to assist health professionals include Web-based online learning courses, audioconferences, Webcasts, PowerPoint presentations, and Web page listings of seminars, symposia, and conferences.

In the private arena, DigiScript <http://bioterrorism.digiscript.com/>, a commercial Web site, is offering free access to several of its commercial educational presentations, including *Responding to Disaster, CDC Clinical Laboratory Response to Bioterrorism*, and *Questions and Answers and ASCP/CAP Bioterrorism Panel in the Bioterrorism Learning Center*. A fairly large calendar of education and training offered by other organizations is provided by the AHA on their disaster readiness Web area at <http://www.aha.org/Emergency/Education/EducationIndex. asp>. The Public Health Foundation offers a distance learning clearinghouse called TrainingFinder.org at <http://www.trainingfinder.org/> that has more than 400 courses and 50 listed with its bioterrorism/emergency preparedness category.

Federally, FEMA's *Compendium of Weapons of Mass Destruction Courses: Sponsored by the Federal Government*, a 160-page PDF document, details federally sponsored NBC (nuclear biologic and chemical) courses from the DOD, DOE, DHHS, FEMA, CSEPP, EMI, NFA, EPA, DOJ, OJP, FBI, and the FBI for training of state and local emergency responders in a "train-the-trainer" design, which can then be tailored locally. See also FEMA's Incident Command System (ICS) self-study online course at <http://www.fema.gov/emi/is195.htm> that is recognized as an effective system for managing emergencies and one that several states have adopted as their standard for emergency management.

Also, the CDC's network of Centers for Public Health Preparedness <http://www.phppo.cdc.gov/owpp/centersforPHP.asp> is a national system for competency-based training for public health professionals and links numerous training partners throughout the U.S., many offering online courses. The CDC training page <http://www.bt.cdc.gov/Training/index.asp> provides PowerPoint slides, Webcasts, and lists of video and satellite broadcasts about bioterrorism. Some CDC education is produced with the University of North Carolina (UNC) School of Public Health on their Web site called *Public Health Grand Rounds: Bioterrorism Implications for Public Health* at <http://www.publichealthgrandrounds.unc.edu/bioterrorism/resources.htm>. The UNC November 2001 Web page update <http://www.publichealthgrandrounds.unc.edu/bioterrorism/resources.htm> includes all CDC and UNC Webcasts on this topic.

On the military side, the U.S. Army Medical Research Institute for Chemical Defense (USAMRICD) Web page, called "Medical Management of Chemical and Biological Casualties" <http://ccc.apgea.army.mil/default.asp>, has links to archives of Web casts and details about training video series and manuals available for purchase. The U.S. Army Medical Research Institute for Infectious Diseases (USAMRIID) education page <http://www.usamriid.army.mil/education/index.html> provides training for biological attacks.

Locally, hospitals may have online presentations or useful documents like an incident command model. Sleuth through your state's hospital Web sites. Although there are Web directories like HospitalWeb, each state hospital association's hospitals directory will provide the most authoritative and comprehensive source of hospital Web links for their state. A directory of links to state hospital associations is at AHA <http://www.aha.org/resource/links.asp#2>. Most of these state associations will offer disaster preparedness and bioterrorism resources as well, many state-specific. One excellent example of a local hospital education program using streaming video is from the Saint Barnabas Health Care System, Livingston, N.J., called *Disaster Preparedness*, by Stuart B. Weiss, MD <http://www.sbhcs.com/news/disaster.html>. National associations also provide training; an example is the American College of Healthcare Executives (ACHE) education page <http://www. ache.org/education.cfm> highlighting its February seminar, "When Disaster Strikes: The Role of the Hospital."

Those wanting to delve further afield or into more specific areas may use, for example, an online Primer on WMD at <http://www.nti.org/ f_wmd411/f_index.html> from the Center for Nonproliferation Studies or its other learning resources at <http://www.cns.miis.edu/cns/edu/ index.htm> or the NLM's Interactive Health Tutorials <http://www.nlm. nih.gov/medlineplus/tutorials.html>, which includes an Anthrax tutorial.

CORE RESOURCES

Key resources for hospital disaster planning, readiness, and training are obvious and not so obvious. Start with those highlighted here and subscribe to the news services listed to keep current as new resources are published. The key resources listed in this article are from voluntary organizations and associations and the federal government. There is no one standard for designing a written hospital disaster plan; however, there are guidelines well-recognized within the field as authoritative, current, and of high quality, some with input from the hospital industry.

Hospital-Specific National Associations

Joint Commission on Accreditation of Healthcare Organizations (JCAHO)
<http://www.jcaho.org/>

The JCAHO Web site offers online purchase of new books, audiocassettes, and other resources for emergency management at <http:// www.jcrinc.com/subscribers/perspectives.asp?durki=1122> and access to JCAHO emergency preparedness consultation and custom education services at <http://www.jcrinc.com/generic.asp?durki=1023>. A key resource is the December 2001 issue of *Joint Commission Perspectives*, free online as a special 24-page issue of the organization's newsletter, covering emergency management in the new millennium. It can be downloaded in its entirety at <http://www.jcrinc.com/subscribers/ images/pubs/pdfs/12-01%20persp.pdf> or selective articles read online. Like a mini-manual with post-September 11 information, it covers the JCAHO standards as a starting point for preparedness, analyzing vulnerability to hazards, and adapting FMECA (failure mode, effect and criticality analysis) for this purpose. It has a complete reprint of the revised *Environment of Care Standards* EC.1.4, from the *Comprehensive Accreditation Manual for Hospitals (CAMH)*. Articles cover development of education programs, preparing for a mass casualty event, emergency and media management checklists, and internal and external crisis communications.

American Hospital Association (AHA)
<http://www.aha.org/index.asp>

The AHA offers an extensive special Web area updated regularly called "Disaster Readiness" <http://www.aha.org/Emergency/EmIndex. asp> with some information offered to AHA members only, password protected. Online resources include news, testimony, advisories, links, and contact information for academic, professional, government, and private organizations, and hotlines. Within the "Resources" area of "Disaster Readiness," three major Web pages offer core online information. The first page, "Government Roles and Planning" <http://www. aha.org/Emergency/Resources/GovernmentRoles.asp>, covers federal, state, and local resources. The second Web page, "Hospital Readiness, Response, Recovery and Outreach" <http://www.aha.org/Emergency/ Resources/HospitalReady.asp>, offers these four titled topics as well as operational resources including checklists, sample plans from hospitals and states, and media and community relations guides. It includes links to regional and state emergency management agencies via a handy chart. An important document included here is the *Hospital Preparedness for Mass Casualties* <http://www.ahapolicyforum.org/policyresources/ MOdisaster.asp>, a final report of the AHA, Office of Emergency Preparedness of the U.S. and the U.S. Department of Health and Human Services. Another important title is the *Mass Casualty Disaster Plan Checklist: A Template for Healthcare Facilities* by APIC and the Center for the Study of Bioterrorism & Emerging Infections. This sixteen-page Word download has no direct URL and is accessible by scrolling down to the title at <http://www.aha.org/Emergency/Resources/HospitalReady. asp>. The third section of the "Resources" area within "Disaster Readiness" is "Guidance for Health Professionals" <http://www. ahapolicyforum.org/policyresources/MOdisaster.asp> with clinical management, diagnosis and treatment, mental health, and laboratory resources. Together, these online resources provide an excellent starting point for evaluating disaster readiness or revising current planning efforts. These AHA selected links, with annotations, pull many core resources together in one central location.

Association for Professionals in Infection Control and Epidemiology, Inc. (APIC)
<http://www.apic.org/>

One of the most important model resources every hospital should have is the *Bioterrorism Readiness Plan: A Template for Healthcare Facilities* created by the APIC Bioterrorism Task Force and the CDC Hospital Infection Program Bioterrorism Working Group. On APIC it is at <http://www.apic.org/educ/readinow.html> or alternatively the CDC at <http://www.cdc.gov/ncidod/hip/Bio/13apr99APIC-CDCBioterrorism. PDF>. This template outlines the steps for response to the most likely biological agents and provides information on the unique characteristics, specific recommendations, management, and follow-up for each. It has an overview of infection control activities, laboratory policy and public inquiry, citations to scientific literature, and useful appendices including contact information for all the FBI field offices, state departments of health and public health directors, and other important telephone numbers. The chapter on bioterrorism from the 2000 edition of the *APIC Text of Infection Control and Epidemiology* <http://www.apic. org/bioterror/chapter124.pdf> is available for free download. Other bioterrorism and readiness resources can be downloaded for free, although they are not easy to find. See also more than fifteen pages of APIC's "Bioterrorism Resources" <http://www.apic.org/bioterror/> covering economic impact, management and treatment, readiness planning, scenarios, reference materials, vaccination, and resources for each biologic warfare agent.

Additional Associations and Organizations

There are countless associations and organizations that offer information about disaster preparedness, bioterrorism, and homeland security. Readers are encouraged to check their state or national professional or trade association as well as state, county, or regional medical societies of the AMA at < http://www.ama-assn.org/ama/pub/article/3958-3926. html>, the schools of medicine at the Association of American Medical Colleges (AAMC) at <http://www.aamc.org/meded/medschls/start.htm>, the schools of public health from the American Public Health Association (APHA) at <http://www.apha.org/public_health/schools.htm>, or APHA's state public health associations at <http://www.apha.org/state_local/>. They all undoubtedly have coverage of this topic to one degree or another, from one critical report or presentation to major Web pages. The following listings highlight a few useful groups for information for hospitals and medical librarians.

The Association of State and Territorial Health Officials (ASTHO) <http://www.astho.org/>

This site offers a "Bioterrorism and Health Alert Network" page <http://www.astho.org/phiip/bioterrorism.html>, and *e-Health*, the association's monthly newsletter <http://www.astho.org/phiip/newsletters.html>, containing extensive links for preparedness, planning, and disease surveillance.

American Medical Association Disaster Preparedness and Medical Response <http://www.ama-assn.org/ama/pub/category/6206.html>

National, state, and physician resources, news, coping with disasters, and free full-text access to *JAMA* articles are available on this topic. An *Index of Bioterrorism Resources* <http://www.ama-assn.org/ama/pub/category/6671.html> is an extensive subject index.

Infectious Diseases Society of America (ISDA) <http://www.idsociety.org/>

ISDA represents physicians, scientists, and other health care professionals who specialize in infectious diseases. The Web site provides a comprehensive "Anthrax Update" <http://www.idsociety.org/NewsRoom/FYI_AnthraxUpdate_11-28-01.htm> using all major scientific sources including the Sverdlovsk outbreak. Its "Bioterrorism Preparedness" page <http://www.idsociety.org/PA/PS&P/BT_Preparedness_10-2-01.htm> extensively answers questions on the topic for infectious disease professionals and offers links to the scholarly literature in *JAMA* on anthrax, smallpox, plague, tularemia, and botulism, along with articles about confronting biological weapons in ISDA's journal, *Clinical Infectious Diseases (CID)*.

Canada. Defense Research Establishment Suffield (DRES)
<http://www.dres.dnd.ca/>

DRES is Canada's main military defense science and technology asset that conducts research to defend against chemical and biological warfare agents. It published a new core scientific research study in September 2001 important for hospitals, offering new science regarding anthrax titled *Risk Assessment of Anthrax Threat Letters* by B. Kournikakis et al., technical report DRES TR-2001-048 <http://www.dres.dnd.ca/Meetings/FirstResponders/tr01-048_annex.pdf>. The report states, "DRES undertook a series of experiments to determine the extent of the hazard. In the experiments, envelopes containing *Bacillus globigii* spores (a stimulant for anthrax) were opened in a mock mail room/office environment. The data measured on the dispersion of the spores were used to estimate if letters containing anthrax spores posed a significant health risk." The risk was catastrophic and previously unknown.[23]

The National Emergency Management Association (NEMA)
<http://nemaweb.org/index.cfm>

NEMA serves state emergency management directors with a Web site of white papers, reports, and news about policy, operations, and strategy. It offers the *HGMP Database* of all disasters searchable by state, disaster, and project types and reports economic costs, year and description.

Federal Government Resources

There are a myriad of government statutes, regulations, and agencies with roles and responsibilities for disasters, preparedness, emergency response, or terrorism and are all-important to hospitals for access to standards, regulations, and current information. The following is a selection of core starting points for federal agencies with an emphasis on areas for preparedness and response; many include standards and regulations.

Centers for Disease Control and Prevention (CDC)
<http://www.cdc.gov>

The CDC site is enormous and finding key areas may be a challenge; nonetheless, content offered is extensive and timely. It's useful to start with the *CDC Prevention Guidelines System* <http://www.phppo.cdc.gov/CDCRecommends/AboutV.asp>. This is a compendium for quick access to the full set of CDC's guidelines from a single point, regardless of where they were originally published.

Next, go to the CDC Public Health Emergency Preparedness & Response site <http://www.bt.cdc.gov/> and then visit the link for its "Preparation and Planning" page <http://www.bt.cdc.gov/Planning/index.asp> for its coverage of national plans and strategies, state and local-level information and plans, health care facilities, legal, and planning issues including quarantines and contacts for preparation and planning. It includes links to other related CDC main sections. The CDC "Emergency Response" page <http://www.bt.cdc.gov/EmContact/index.asp> provides emergency notification procedures for state and local officials and health care providers, along with a 24-hour contact number.

For laboratories, the CDC offers two areas. One, the "Lab Information" pages <http://www.bt.cdc.gov/LabIssues/index.asp>, offers overviews, testing, and presumptive agent identification, biosafety, shipping specimens, regulations and training. The "Lab & Health Professionals" pages <http://www.bt.cdc.gov/HealthProfessionals/index.asp> provide agents and threats, news and investigations, and preparation and planning. The PowerPoint presentation at <http://www.phppo.cdc.gov/nltn/pdf/LRN99.pdf> describes the Laboratory Response Network for Bioterrorism (LRN) and each type of laboratory, how to access the State Public Health Laboratory, the Centers for Disease Control and Prevention, and the FBI to refer or report suspected agents.

The CDC's National Immunization Program "Smallpox" home page <http://www.cdc.gov/nip/smallpox/> provides the *Interim Smallpox Guidelines and Response Plan* <http://www.bt.cdc.gov/DocumentsApp/Smallpox/RPG/index.asp> and Web pages for health care providers at <http://www.cdc.gov/nip/smallpox/Providers.htm> offering evaluation, training, and resources. The National Pharmaceutical Stockpile Web page <http://www.cdc.gov/nceh/nps/default.htm> is part of CDC's National Center for Environmental Health. The NPS ensures the availability and rapid deployment of life-saving pharmaceuticals, antidotes, other medical supplies, and equipment necessary to combat the nerve agents, biological pathogens, and chemical agents and is ready immediately when needed. This page provides a complete overview for hospitals. The CDC's National Electronic Disease Surveillance System <http://www.cdc.gov/od/hissb/act_int.htm> will allow the public health community to respond more quickly to public health threats before they are epidemics by electronically integrating over 100 CDC surveillance systems. This Web page describes the system under development and links to key documents.

Last but not least, the CDC Web site for the *Morbidity and Mortality Weekly Report (MMWR)* <http://www.cdc.gov/mmwr/> offers the latest guidance on biologic warfare agents such as anthrax.

U.S. Department of Health and Human Services, Office of Emergency Preparedness (HHS/OEP) and the National Disaster Medical System (NDMS)
<http://ndms.dhhs.gov>

The HHS/OEP is the lead agency within the Federal Response Plan that manages and coordinates federal health, medical, and health related social services and recovery for major emergencies and federally declared disasters. OEP also directs the National Disaster Medical System (NDMS) <http://ndms.dhhs.gov/NDMS/ndms.html>, a partnership between HHS, the Department of Defense (DOD), the Department of Veterans Affairs (VA), FEMA, state and local governments, private businesses, and civilian volunteers. Their roles are to coordinate federal health and medical response to terrorist acts involving WMD. OEP manages the Metropolitan Medical Response System (MMRS) <http://www.mmrs.hhs.gov/Index.cfm> that includes more than 70 cities with systems in place working to develop coordinated response (fire, police, EMS, hospital, public health,) to WMD incidents. A map with names of each MMRS is located at <http://www.mmrs.hhs.gov/Pub/About/ProDesc.cfm>. The Web site provides a searchable database of documents developed by all participants browseable by category that includes emergency medical services, hospital operations, laboratories, and mental health services. A concise guide to the HHS role for disasters and terrorism and the NDMS can be found at <http://www.hhs.gov/news/press/2001pres/01fsemergencyresponse.html>.

National Library of Medicine (NLM)
<http://www.nlm.nih.gov/>

The PubMed database <http://www.ncbi.nlm.nih.gov/entrez/query.fcgi> is the key source for searches of the journal literature in the health care field. PubMed is searchable with text words as well as controlled vocabulary called MeSH (Medical Subject Headings). Key MeSH terms are disasters, disaster planning, natural disasters, bioterrorism (entered in 2001), biological warfare, chemical warfare, nuclear war-

fare, chemical warfare agents. Use the MeSH browser <http://www.
ncbi.nlm.nih.gov/entrez/meshbrowser.cgi> to find more vocabulary for
specific types of disasters and chemical warfare agents.

Much of the NLM Web site focuses on clinicians and consumers. However, some of this general information is of use for preparedness and medical library services to patients and the community. Key Web pages for this
purpose are from MEDLINEplus, "Biological and Chemical Weapons"
<http://www.nlm.nih.gov/medlineplus/biologicalandchemicalweapons.
html> and "Disasters and Emergency Preparedness" <http://www.nlm.
nih.gov/medlineplus/disastersandemergencypreparedness.html>. For the
professional, two of NLM's Specialized Information Services (SIS)
Web pages are "Biological Warfare" <http://sis.nlm.nih.gov/Tox/
biologicalwarfare.htm> and SIS "Chemical Warfare Agents" <http://
sis.nlm.nih.gov/Tox/ChemWar.html>. The latter includes PubMed links
to select journal literature and a TOXLINE search for review articles
about chemical warfare agents, likewise with PubMed article links.

The Toxicology and Environmental Health Web portal <http://sis.
nlm.nih.gov/Tox/ToxMain.html> offers TOXNET (Toxicology Data
Network) access at <http://toxnet.nlm.nih.gov/>, toxicology tutorials,
publications, PowerPoint lecture guides, news, and training events.
TOXNET is a cluster of eleven databases for four main areas covering
facts on toxicity and hazards, the toxicology literature, toxic releases
and chemical nomenclature and structures. The literature areas cover
biochemical, pharmacological, physiological, and toxicological effects
of drugs and other chemicals.

Occupational Safety & Health Administration (OSHA)
<http://www.osha.gov/>

Hospitals need to comply with OSHA regulations, and warfare
agents involved in a disaster pose special concerns. Information includes
Protecting the Worksite Against Terrorism: Anthrax <http://www.osha.
gov/bioterrorism/anthrax/index.html>, *Occupational Exposure to Anthrax OSHA's FAQs* <http://www.osha.gov/bioterrorism/anthrax/faqs.
html>, and *Risk Reduction Matrix* <http://www.osha.gov/bioterrorism/
anthrax/matrix/index.html>. The HAZWOPER Web page <http://
www.osha-slc.gov/html/faq-hazwoper.html> covers the *Hazardous
Waste Operations and Emergency Response Standard*, its training requirements for hospital staff and reference interpretation, and compliance for physicians, nurses, hospital, and medical personnel. A core
text, *Hospitals and Community Emergency Response: What You Need*

to Know, is online at <http://www.osha-slc.gov/Publications/OSHA3152/ osha3152.html> and covers planning, standards, legal requirements, and guidance for what to include in a hospital disaster plan.

Federal Emergency Management Agency (FEMA) <http://www.fema.gov/>

In 1979, President Carter established FEMA after the Three Mile Island Nuclear Generating Station incident, and in 1980 amendments to the Civil Defense Act mandated the agency to work with state and local governments to assist in setting up emergency management programs.[21] The FEMA site thus offers important information for the local planner and includes an "Emergency Managers" page <http://www.fema.gov/ emanagers/> with useful guidance, links, and national situation updates. To learn how FEMA works on the state and local level for understanding coordination and communication within the context of hospital disaster planning, use its text, *State and Local Guide (SLG) 101: Guide for All-Hazard Emergency Operations Planning* <http://www.fema.gov/ pte/gaheop.htm>. See chapter 5 for planning guidance for health and medical functions and revised chapter 6 for terrorism. All chapters are available as PDF documents. For a directory of FEMA regional and area offices see <http://www.fema.gov/about/regoff.htm>.

Food and Drug Administration (FDA) <http://www.fda.gov/oc/opacom/hottopics/bioterrorism.html>

The FDA site is an authoritative source for anthrax drug treatment, anthrax vaccine, and drug preparedness, the latter under its public health initiatives section. Consumer information is also provided, useful for a hospital's community health and outreach with topics such as bogus bioterrorism products, the difference between anthrax and the flu, how to handle suspicious letters, and should you buy Cipro® or other antibiotics. All are ready to print and make available to the public.

Environmental Protection Agency (EPA) <http://www.epa.gov/>

At the EPA site a key page is "Emergencies" <http://www.epa.gov/ ebtpages/emergencies.html>. From here additional topics can be viewed for counterterrorism, emergency preparedness, emergency response, and others. EPA has a Chemical Emergency Prevention and Preparedness office and Web site at <http://www.epa.gov/swercepp/index.html> offering Web topical pages for prevention, preparedness, response, and counterterrorism that includes the Emergency Planning and Community Right-to-Know Act as well as links to sources of chemical data.

Agency for Toxic Substances and Disease Registry (ATSDR) <http://www.atsdr.cdc.gov/mmg.html>

This Web site offers guidelines called *Medical Management Guidelines for Acute Chemical Exposures* to aid emergency care professionals and is also useful for disaster planning. It covers all aspects of patient management including decontamination, protection, communication, and transportation.

Office for Domestic Preparedness <http://www.ojp.usdoj.gov/odp/>

As part of the U.S. Department of Justice, the ODP provides resources of interest for readiness. The PDF of the text *Critical Incident Protocol: A Public Private Partnership, 2000* by Michigan State University <http://www.ojp.usdoj.gov/odp/docs/cip.pdf> is not a checklist but a set of protocols for community planning for emergencies whether of minor or WMD scale and covers mitigation, recovery, lessons learned, best practices, and exercises. For health professionals, it's useful for understanding how to develop partnerships and how disasters affect the community that the hospital serves.

Office of Homeland Security <http://www.whitehouse.gov/homeland/>

For a national perspective, this Web site of the White House describes the mission and activities of this office and links to the Executive Order for its establishment. Presently, its value is in the links it offers for federal information and current news on terrorism.

National Domestic Preparedness Office (NDPO) <http://www.ndpo.gov/>

Within the Federal Bureau of Investigation, the NDPO is a clearinghouse for information and assistance with weapons of mass destruction and covers medical and health responders. Its health and medical services program <http://www.ndpo.gov/services.htm> provides articles, training aids, and research information for the emergency response community. Another resource is *The Beacon* <http://www.ndpo.gov/beacon.htm>, a newsletter by and for emergency responders.

Department of Transportation (DOT) Office of Hazardous Materials Safety
<http://hazmat.dot.gov/>

The Web site provides more than twenty topics linked via colorful HAZMAT signs easy to overlook as simple graphics. Importantly, it offers extensive guidelines for transporting anthrax and anthrax-contaminated objects and materials at <http://hazmat.dot.gov/guide_anthrax.htm>.

National Guideline Clearinghouse™ (NGC)
<http://www.guideline.gov>

The National Guideline Clearinghouse is sponsored by the U.S. Agency for Healthcare Research and Quality. There is a series of evidence-based guidelines on anthrax and other biological agents within this site at <http://www.guideline.gov/STATIC/bio.asp?view=bio>.

United States General Accounting Office. Special Collections: Terrorism
<http://www.gao.gov/terrorism.html>

This is a comprehensive listing of more than 100 GAO reports on this topic, updated daily. It includes numerous reports on medical readiness, preparedness, and bioterrorism.

United States Department of State. Response to Terrorism
<http://usinfo.state.gov/topical/pol/terror/>

This comprehensive Web site covers national policy, is available in six languages, includes key documents and in depth subject reviews, and lists the designated terrorist organizations. It provides "The Network of Terrorism" <http://usinfo.state.gov/products/pubs/netterror.htm>, which is a factual summary of what is known about the terrorist attacks of September 11 and their connection to Osama bin Laden and his al Qaida terrorist network and is very helpful to dispel or confirm rumors.

State Government Resources

Valuable resources and local homeland security information are located on state government sites. One example is the *Hospital Emergency Incident Command System (HEICS)*, developed by the San Mateo County (CA) Department of Health, and a key resource for disaster readiness, recommended by the AHA as an "effective disaster readiness tool."[22] It can be downloaded in several formats at <http://www.emsa.cahwnet.gov/dms2/download.htm>. A quick chart of all state emergency management agencies can be found on AHA's *Other Operational Resources* <http://www.aha.org/Emergency/Resources/HospitalReady.asp#Operational>. Also, ASTHO's *State/Territorial Links* page <http://www.astho.org/state.html> links to all departments of health. HAL, the Health Agency Locator <http://www.statepublichealth.org/index.php> from StatePublicHealth.org is sponsored by ASTHO and the National Governors Association. HAL is a comprehensive series of several online directories and public health hotlines.

Military

There are several books that hospitals should have readily available to be prepared for any terrorist event. First is *Medical Management of Biological Casualties Handbook*, fourth edition, February 2001, available at <http://www.usamriid.army.mil/education/bluebook.html> with choices of several formats, including PDF, PALM OS, and Word. Second is the *Textbook of Military Medicine: Medical Aspects of Chemical & Biological* Warfare <http://ccc.apgea.army.mil/reference_materials/textbook/HTML_Restricted/index.htm>. A third volume is *The Medical Management of Chemical Casualties Handbook*, third edition, 1999 <http://ccc.apgea.army.mil/reference_materials/handbooks/RedHandbook/001TitlePage.htm>; and finally, *The Medical Management of Radiological Casualties*, first edition, December 1999 <http://www.afrri.usuhs.mil/www/outreach/pdf/radiologicalhandbooksp99-2.pdf>. The Medical NBC Online Information Server (NBC-MED) <http://www.nbc-med.org/others/Default.html> is invaluable and offers extensive medical resources, training, and news.

Private, Academic, or Think Tanks

GovStar Disaster and Emergency Management Web Resources
<http://govstar.com/>

GovStar is run by the Tahoe Internet Corporation as a public service information portal for federal, state, and local governmental information and public risk management. This one portal for disaster and emergencies covers nine areas as follows: terrorism, biochemicals, cyber crimes, disaster management, emergency management, emergency medical, hazardous materials, natural hazards and security, a discussion forum, and document library.

Center for Civilian Biodefense Strategies, Johns Hopkins University
<http://www.hopkins-biodefense.org/index.html>

This site is sponsored by the Alfred P. Sloan Foundation and the Robert Wood Johnson Foundation. Its purpose is to build a knowledge base and foster planning and preparation for response to possible bioterrorist attacks. Resources offered include biologic agent information, a library, and news. An example of resources is the article published online, by Thomas A. Glass and Monica Schoch-Spana, "Bioterrorism and the People: How to Vaccinate a City Against Panic," *Clinical Infectious Diseases* 34 (2002): 217-223. It offers five guidelines for increasing the involvement of the public at <http://www.journals.uchicago.edu/CID/journal/issues/v34n2/011333/011333.html>.

Center for Nonproliferation Studies Monterey Institute of International Studies
<http://www.cns.miis.edu/>

This is the world's largest non-governmental organization devoted to combating the spread of WMD with an expansive selection of resources on public policy as well as operational insights for readiness including a library, databases, books, testimony, and Web reports to name a few. It can be browsed by geographic region or topic, with the latter including terrorism, biological, chemical, and nuclear.

Center for the Study of Bioterrorism and Emerging Infections, Saint Louis University School of Public Health
<http://bioterrorism.slu.edu/>

This site offers case studies, bibliographies, fact sheets, and much more. It includes annotated Internet links for professional association resources at <http://bioterrorism.slu.edu/internet/professional.htm> and academic resources for bioterrorism at <http://bioterrorism.slu.edu/internet/academic.htm>.

The National Academies: Terrorism and Security Collection
<http://www.nap.edu/terror/index.html>

The Academies site <http://www.nationalacademies.org> includes the Institute of Medicine. This special collection links 26 recent books about the science and policy issues surrounding terrorism and security, which can be read and searched online for free at <http://www.nap.edu/terror/index.html>. It includes the titles *Chemical and Biological Terrorism: Research and Development to Improve Civilian Medical Response, Fluid Resuscitation: State of the Science for Treating Combat Casualties and Civilian Injuries*, and *Firepower in the Lab*. The "Medicine and Public Health" topic page <http://books.nap.edu/v3/makepage.phtml?val1=subject&val2=ms> includes more online books related to disasters, preparedness, and bioterrorism.

ANSER Institute for Homeland Security
<http://www.homelandsecurity.org/>

This nonprofit public services research institute partners with other nonprofits and academic institutions. ANSER has no formal relationship with the federal government or the White House Office of Homeland Security. It is an excellent comprehensive resource for public policy, research and news, training courses, legislation, links, briefings, and reports. It has a unique "Notable Quotes" Web area <http://www.homelandsecurity.org/quotes/quote.cfm> for extensive quotations from public, private, military, government, and congressional sources useful for presentations. The "Homeland Security State and Local Resources" page <http://www.homelandsecurity.org/bulletin/statepages.htm> notes new activities at this level with links to sources.

World Health Organization (WHO)
<http://www.who.int/home-page/>

WHO covers fourteen infectious diseases and warfare agents worldwide and reports on outbreaks and biosafety. Its "Communicable Disease Surveillance and Response" (CDSR) site <http://www.who.int/emc/questions.htm> answers frequently asked questions about the deliberate use of chemical and biological weapons. The "Health Aspects of Biological and Chemical Weapons" page <http://www.who.int/emc/deliberate_epi.html> provides all the WHO reports published on this topic.

The Terrorism Research Center
<http://www.terrorism.com/index.shtml>

This site is the next generation of terrorism analysis, used by the media and an independent organization without a particular political slant. It provides general terrorism news, analysis, counterterrorism resources, training, consultation, profiles of terrorist groups, a calendar of significant dates related to terrorism, travel advisories, and extensive Internet links.

News Services, Electronic Newsletters, Journals

AHA NewsNow.com
<http://www.ahanews.com>

This is a free daily online newsletter (*AHA News* is a paper weekly companion piece). It is a comprehensive source of hospital and health care news stories including disaster preparedness and bioterrorism. To register, go to <http://www.ahanews.com/asp/getnewnow.asp> and view the current edition at <http://www.ahanews.com/default.asp>.

Web Extra: Disaster Readiness
<http://www.hhnmag.com>

Many of the articles on disaster readiness from five of AHA's magazines are available at no charge and include *Hospitals and Health Networks, Materials Management in Health Care, Trustee* and *Health Forum* <http://www.hhnmag.com/asp/ArticleDisplay.asp?PubID=1&ArticleID=15984>.

AMNews American Medical Association
<http://www.ama-assn.org/public/journals/amnews>

This newspaper, called *American Medical News* in its paper format and *AMNews* for the electronic version, offers ongoing coverage of September 11, the medical response, how the aftermath is affecting health care, biothreats, and preparedness. All of the articles appear on its "Special Coverage" Web page in the topic "Terrorism in America" <http://www.ama-assn.org/public/journals/amnews/amnspecial.htm#terror>.

Southern Medical Journal
<http://www.sma.org/smj/fulltext.htm>

The full-text article archive covers 1996 through 2001. See the June 1997 issue for a core reference: Sadayoshi Ohbu et al. "Sarin Poisoning on Tokyo Subway," *Southern Medical Journal* 90(6) at <http://www.sma.org/smj/97juntoc.htm>. It describes the terrorist incident, classifying the injured, laboratory data, hospital deployment, post-incident symptoms, secondary contamination at hospital, discussion, and references.

NewScientist.com Hot Topics: Bioterrorism and Bioweapons Special Report
<http://www.newscientist.com/hottopics/bioterrorism/>

This is the Web site of the magazine *NewScientist*. It pulls into one location all the news articles it has published with links on the topic. It also offers a weekly *New Scientist Newsletter* outlining key stories from the print edition and the *New Scientist Compendium*, a quarterly round up of the humorous top stories, offering a break from the disaster and bioterror topics.

EIIP Virtual Forum–*Emergency Partner Posting Newsletter*
<http://www.emforum.org/eiip/news.htm>
and the EIIP Mail Lists
<http://www.emforum.org/vforum/maillist.htm>

The monthly newsletter covers the world of emergency management and disaster response with updates on activities and services available through the Emergency Information Infrastructure Partnership (EIIP) Virtual Forum <http://www.emforum.org/index.html>. It offers a current list of seminars, conferences, and training events from participants, electronic sources, and articles. There are several listservs, and those of interest to hospitals include *CFP* for community preparedness and *Forum,* covering all phases and sectors involved with disasters.

The Journal of Homeland Security
<http://www.homelandsecurity.org/journal/>

Published weekly with an electronic e-mail alert by ANSER, this journal is consistently of high quality and offers substantive interviews with key individuals in the field, book reviews, science and technology, and original articles.

Homeland Security Newsletter
<http://www.homelandsecurity.org/journal/HLDBulletin/dsp_Bul letinForm.cfm>

Published weekly by ANSER, this newsletter uses an e-mail alert service to update the reader to new items on the ANSER Institute Web site. The current bulletin is at <http://www.homelandsecurity.org/ bulletin/current_bulletin.htm>.

TRC Real News

This free electronic news clipping service for the major newspapers provides links to stories specifically on bioterrorism, homeland security, and related topics. To register, go to <http://www.terrorism.com/ mail/subscribe.asp>.

ALGORITHM
FOR DISASTER INFORMATION PREPAREDNESS:
CHECKLIST FOR MEDICAL LIBRARIANS

This algorithm offers basic steps to assure a medical library is prepared to support the information needs of clinicians and patients in the event of a biochemical attack or disaster. It should be supplemented and revised initially and regularly based on your local needs, the emergency response plan of your health facility, and any special facility plans for biochemical terrorism.

Secure Clinical Resources for Bioterrorism, Mass Casualties and Disasters

A medical librarian should use Internet and Web resources provided here to assist the parent health care facility adequately prepare and remain up-to-date with the ever-changing field. Additionally, the medical librarian should also plan for the clinical information needs and resources during a disaster or a terrorist event using bioterrorism resources mentioned in this volume. See also the clinical resources from the December 5, 2001 seminar, *Thinking the Unthinkable–Biochemical Terrorism and Disasters: Resources for Medical Librarians* <http://www.njha.com/njresponse/biopresent.asp>, sponsored by the New Jersey Hospital Association and the Middle Atlantic Region of the National Network/Libraries of Medicine. All of the seminar's PowerPoint presentations and handouts by the speakers from the CDC, NLM and USAMRICD are online and contain active Web links and thus become concise authoritative mini-manuals to clinical information resources for these topics. With all of this information the librarian can then apply this knowledge, reviewing this checklist and developing a written plan.

Boolean Algorithm of Key Concepts of Medical Library Preparedness

For summary purposes, this algorithm can be expressed as a Boolean search statement as follows and considers these main disaster planning components: (Planned Improvisation + Training + Documentation) ADJ (Communication + Coordination) </> Readiness ≅ Implementation.

Planned Improvisation

Remember, in these unprecedented times, this checklist is solely a starting point for further development of a comprehensive local plan for a medical library's information preparedness for biochemical disasters. Importantly, when implemented, disaster planning, whether for a library or a hospital, needs to use planned improvisation. This is the ability to improvise in a planned and coordinated manner for any one of a series of biochemical events, based on the written established medical library information response plan, allowing coherent action regardless of the type or scale of disaster, since not all can be predicted and documented.

The Checklist, Carpe Diem

With hindsight, it is apparent why Noah built the Ark before the flood! The *Checklist* shown as the Appendix was created based on actual experiences during two weeks of library services beginning with the events of September 11, in disaster-mode. This checklist is offered to help medical librarians before another disaster or terrorist attack; it will be periodically updated at <http://www.njha.com/njresponse/pdf/ bio-NJHAhandout.pdf> and suggestions for this purpose can be made to the author. The *Checklist* is reprinted with the permission of the New Jersey Hospital Association.

CONCLUSION

To conclude, this quote by D.A. Henderson, Director, Johns Hopkins Center for Civilian Defense sums up the importance of learning these resources, of hospital disaster preparedness and the necessity for the checklist. Take action, knowing the storm ahead.

> Specialists in infectious diseases thus constitute the front line of defense. The rapidity with which they and emergency room personnel reach a proper diagnosis and the speed with which they apply preventive and therapeutic measures could spell the difference between thousands and perhaps tens of thousands of casualties. Indeed, the survival of physicians and health-care staff caring for the patients may be at stake. However, today few have ever seen so much as a single case of smallpox, plague, or anthrax, or, for that matter, would recall the characteristics of such cases.[24]

NOTES

1. Erik Auf der Heide, "Designing a Disaster Plan: Important Questions," *Plant Technology and Safety Management Series* PTSM no. 3, (1994): 12, 14.

2. American Hospital Association, "What to Tell Your Community About Anthrax," *Readiness Bulletin* (October 19, 2001). Available: <http://www.aha.org/ Emergency/Readiness/RbAlertB1018.asp>.

3. Joint Commission on Accreditation of Healthcare Organizations, "Standards Revisions for 2001 EC.1.4 Emergency Management." Available: <http://www.jcaho.org/standards_frm.html>.

4. Joint Commission on Accreditation of Healthcare Organizations, "Surveyors to Focus on Emergency Management, Staffing Effectiveness," *JCAHOnline* (January 2002). Available: <http://www.jcaho.org/tip/j_online0102.html>.

5. N.J.A.C. 8:43G-5.16.

6. National Library of Medicine, "Specialized Information Services: Biological Warfare." Available: <http://sis.nlm.nih.gov/Tox/biologicalwarfare.htm>.

7. National Library of Medicine, "Specialized Information Services: Chemical Warfare Agents." Available: <http://sis.nlm.nih.gov/Tox/ChemWar.html>.

8. Op. cit. Erik Auf der Heide: 7.

9. Lawrence K. Altman and Gina Kolata, "Anthrax Missteps Offer Guide to Fight Next Bioterror Battle," *The New York Times* 151(51, 1990):1.

10. Ibid.

11. New Jersey Hospital Association, "Emergency Assistance Update September 12, 2001 11:30 a.m." Available: <http://www.njha.com/njresponse/njresponse.html>.

12. New Jersey Hospital Association, New Jersey Department of Health and Senior Services and the Medical Society of New Jersey, "Ten Things You Should Know About Anthrax," November 16, 2001. Available: <http://www.njha.com/njresponse/pdf/AnthraxFacts.pdf>.

13. The ANSER Institute for Homeland Security, "Notable Quotes," January 24, 2001. Available: <http://www.homelandsecurity.org/quotes/quote.cfm?Authorid=42>.

14. The 6th Annual Emergency Medical Preparedness Symposium, September 11-13, 2001, Holiday Inn, Albany, N.Y. Available: <http://www.va.gov/visns/visn02/emp/emergency/emerprep2001.pdf>.

15. Jerry L. Mothershead, "Introduction to Disaster Planning: The Scope and Nature of the Problem," *eMedicine Journal* 2, no. 7 (July 2, 2001). Available: <http://www.emedicine.com/emerg/topic718.htm>.

16. Kristi L. Koenig. "Describing Disasters: A New Nomenclature," *Plant Technology and Safety Management Series* PTSM no. 3, (1994): 19.

17. Joint Commission on Accreditation of Healthcare Organizations. "Standards Revisions for 2001 EC.1.4 Emergency Management." Available: <http://www.jcaho.org/standards_frm.html>.

18. The ANSER Institute for Homeland Security, "Executive Summary," in *Homeland Security: Balancing a National Strategy Prevention & Deterrence*, (February 11, 2000). Available: <http://www.homelandsecurity.org/FRExecSum.cfm>.

19. Slee's *Health Care Terms eEdition*, 4th edition. Saint Paul, MN: Tringa Press, October 2001. Available: <http://www.tringa.com/index.php>.

20. "What the Survey Process Expects of Your Organization," *Joint Commission Perspectives* 21, no. 12 (December 2001): 6. Available: <http://www.jcrinc.com/subscribers/perspectives.asp?durki=1006&site=10&return=1122>.

21. N.J. Office of Emergency Management, "Press Room: Emergency Management in New Jersey A Historical Perspective. " Available: <http://www.state.nj.us/njoem/press_emhistory.html>.

22. "Hospital Association Recommends HEICS for Disaster Readiness," *Healthcare Security and Disaster Alert* 1, no. 1 (December 2001): 12.

23. Lawrence K. Altman and Gina Kolata, op. cit.

24. D.A. Henderson, "Bioterrorism as a Public Health Threat," *Emerging Infectious Diseases*, 4, no. 3 (July-September 1998). Available: <http://www.cdc.gov/ncidod/eid/vol4no3/hendrsn.htm>.

APPENDIX

Algorithm for Disaster Information Preparedness: Checklist for Medical Librarians–Revised 12/21/01

Personal

Assure personal safety and disaster readiness

- ❑ Family planning and communications.
- ❑ Access preparedness information from the American Red Cross <http://www.redcross.org/services/disaster/beprepared/> and FEMA <http://www.fema.gov/dizprepare.htm> Web sites.
- ❑ Charge your cell phone regularly.
- ❑ _____
- ❑ _____

Professional

Assumptions

- ❑ Facility is part of what local or regional public health system for disaster response, what support does this provide?
- ❑ How ready is the facility for biochemical disasters, status of facility-wide planning efforts?
- ❑ What support does the medical library have for information preparedness, what additional information may be needed in this regard?
- ❑ What is the information system's disaster and contingency plan and how does this impact your system-based resources and services? Consider these implications in areas that follow.
- ❑ _____
- ❑ _____
- ❑ _____

Chain of Command

- ❑ Review facility's emergency response plan, your role.
- ❑ Who is your facility's designated disaster preparedness and/or bioterrorism key emergency contact(s)? Can you define core teams you need to be aware of?

- Identify lines of authority and key individuals for disasters and biochemical incidents, document.
- Create e-mail groups and paper lists of chains/contacts/teams.
- Consider primary, secondary and tertiary communication groups for communication of library resources, actions and services both within and external of medical library.
- Is key staff aware of your home and cell phone numbers?
- _____
- _____
- _____

Needs/Resources/Services

- Assess local information needs for biochemical information
  - Textbooks, journals
  - Research sources, databases
  - Multimedia
  - News services
  - Graphics: Pictures, Photographs, Radiographs, etc.
  - Translation Services
  - Training on information sources
  - Resources for PALM or other PDA formats.
  - _____
  - _____
  - _____
- Inventory existing locally owned information resources for biochemical disasters.
- Inventory existing Web-accessible information resources for biochemical disasters.
- Identify budget or secure additional funding needed.
- Determine priorities, select new resources needed for purchase.
- Intranet access for library's biochemical disaster resources or other local information access.
- Establish new services as required; consider an internal library listserv for staff specifically for this purpose.
- Establish information triage plan for biochemical disaster and non-biochemical disaster information needs, plan back-up staffing as needed.
- Do you have a "buddy system" in place in the event local electronic resources are inaccessible?

APPENDIX (continued)

- ❑ _____
- ❑ _____
- ❑ _____

Training

- ❑ Assess professional training needs of yourself and library staff.
- ❑ Budget for and attend library-training programs.
- ❑ Assess/create training syllabus for clinician's use of biochemical disaster information resources.
- ❑ _____
- ❑ _____
- ❑ _____

Documentation

- ❑ **Identify and document local, state and national contacts 24-hour emergency information**
  - ❑ Document all items listed on checklist as part of medical library's information preparedness plan, in both electronic and print formats.
  - ❑ Print key intranet resources and bookmarks in paper and diskette backup (i.e., non-servers).
  - ❑ Locate plan, intranet resources and bookmarks in three places, with at least one location not local.
  - ❑ _____
  - ❑ _____
  - ❑ _____
  - ❑ Annually review and revise plan.

Communication

- ❑ **Establish need for plan with executive or manager to whom library director reports;** communicate final plan priorities.
- ❑ Create plan's legitimacy with potential users via agreement for need of plan; draft plan for their review and approval.
- ❑ Clearly communicate with library staff the plan, library staffs' priorities, responsibilities and lines of authority during a biochemical disaster.
- ❑ Share your information readiness plan with key groups listed in "chain of command."
- ❑ Market biochemical information resource, training, services and access to users.
- ❑ Determine best method to periodically inform/remind users of information resources for biochemical disasters.

- Communicate via listservs as needed or create/use new listserv service specifically for this purpose.
- _____
- _____
- _____

Coordination

- Coordinate information preparedness activities with key biochemical disaster staff as needed.
- Determine in advance what actions and activities of the medical library need coordination with key staff during a biochemical disaster.
- If coordination meetings occur during a biochemical disaster response, provide the latest printed materials as needed at each meeting.
- Post biochemical disaster incident; provide summary of medical library response and support.
- Coordinate activities with the library's local, regional or state consortia as needed.
- _____
- _____
- _____

Miscellaneous–During Biochemical Disaster

- Determine key authoritative, high quality updated Web site or contact for *local* information on specific disaster event and communicate to key staff. This will differ for each event and should be evaluated as event occurs. Change as needed.
- Remember the human element and adjust accordingly; don't underestimate the traumatic and stressful responses that occur by everyone. Acknowledge emotions without judgment.
- Remember telephones and Internet access may be disabled temporarily or occasionally.
- As needed, establish medical library as formal or informal response for verification of information rumors or hoaxes using standard information skills.
- Determine library staffing needed during biochemical disaster.
- Determine if triage plan for information requests is needed and implement, communicate with users if plan is or is not in effect.
- Create one filing area for all library records and ready reference for biochemical disaster requests, especially if routine reshelving, etc., needs to be suspended for the duration of the disaster.

"HOT" BIBLIOGRAPHIES

Deborah A. Curry, "Hot" Bibliographies Editor

News Sites:
Locating News as It Happens

M. Sandra Wood

SUMMARY. People worldwide rely on the news media to report current events accurately and without bias. TV and radio have been available for decades to report the news, but the Internet is rapidly becoming a major source for instantaneous news. During and following the events of September 11, users with access to the Internet watched the terrorist attacks of September unfold and have continued to watch and monitor the "War on Terrorism" via the Internet. This column presents a highly select list of Web sites that generate current news information; news about September 11 and the War on Terrorism is featured. *[Article copies available for a fee from The Haworth Document Delivery Service: 1-800-HAWORTH. E-mail address: <getinfo@haworthpressinc.com> Website: <http://www. HaworthPress.com> © 2002 by The Haworth Press, Inc. All rights reserved.]*

M. Sandra Wood (mswood@psu.edu) is Librarian, Reference and Database Services, George T. Harrell Library, Milton S. Hershey Medical Center, Pennsylvania State University, Box 850, Hershey, PA 17033-0850.

[Haworth co-indexing entry note]: "News Sites: Locating News as It Happens." Wood, Sandra M. Co-published simultaneously in *Internet Reference Services Quarterly* (The Haworth Information Press, an imprint of The Haworth Press, Inc.) Vol. 6, No. 3/4, 2002, pp. 133-137; and: *Bioterrorism and Political Violence: Web Resources* (ed: M. Sandra Wood) The Haworth Information Press, an imprint of The Haworth Press, Inc., 2002, pp. 133-137. Single or multiple copies of this article are available for a fee from The Haworth Document Delivery Service [1-800-HAWORTH, 9:00 a.m. - 5:00 p.m. (EST). E-mail address: getinfo@haworthpressinc. com].

133

KEYWORDS. News sites, news services, September 11, War on Terrorism, Internet

As the events of September 11 unfolded, many Americans, and others around the world, watched the second plane strike the World Trade Tower live, on television. Events of the day were carried live on television, as they happened. Others, like myself, at work that day and without access to TV, went online and watched the events live via real-time video from news sites on the Internet. While many sites have emerged that cover the events of September 11, the anthrax scare, and the War on Terrorism, the best place to find up-to-date information remains the international and network TV news sites on the Internet. Local television stations link to their national network sites or to international news agencies, providing another avenue of access to these sites. Internet sites such as Netscape maintain their own news information, but much of the content is derived from other sources. This column focuses only on a few selected sites that form a core of locations for current news, most of which have archived information and ongoing stories related to September 11 and the War on Terrorism.

NEWS SITES

ABC News.com
<http://www.abcnews.com/>

The ABC News.com site has links to News Summaries, U.S. News, International News, ESPN Sports, and more. The home page also includes current headlines, video and audio clips, and financial information. The search feature on the site appears to be the only way to get to older news stories. When logging onto this site, using either <http://www.abcnews.com> or <http://www.abcnews.go.com/index.html>, you had to view an advertisement of the day. This "login" ad plus pop-up ads was annoying.

Associated Press
<http://www.ap.org>

The Associated Press "is a not-for-profit cooperative . . . owned by its 1,550 U.S. daily newspaper members." The AP news feeds serve over

10,000 newspapers in the U.S. and worldwide along with radio and TV stations in 112 countries. "The Wire" can be localized to news generated for AP member sites.

CBS News.com
<http://www.cbsnews.com>

The CBS News site includes links to its news programs (The Early Show, 48 Hours, 60 Minutes, CBS Evening News) across the top of the home page. Links down the left side of the page include "Interactives," national news, world news, health, sports, and weather. From the home page, choose either "America Fights Back Complete Coverage" or "Special Report, War on Terror." Both lead to the "War on Terror" page, which has current news stories. From this page, you can link into an interactive window on "Terror Hits Home" (part I) and "The Retaliation" (part II).

CNN.com
<http://www.cnn.com>

The CNN Web site features current news, with sections on the world, U.S., politics, health, sports, education, and more; information about what's on CNN TV; video clips of news events, and a business/money section. A link to the "War Against Terror" is available on the home page. Selecting this takes you to an in-depth special page with "Top Stories" about breaking news; "Background" stories, which include everything from paps and 3D models to overview articles and photo galleries; and an "Archive" of stories and video. Also from this page are links to "America at Home," "Front Lines," "Bin Laden," "Afghanistan," "Anthrax," "Victims," and "September 11." The September 11 link goes to a page, "Day of Terror," that includes everything from a chronology and personal accounts to video of the day's events.

Fox News Channel
<http://www.foxnews.com>

Fox News online features current news stories and includes links to politics, business, weather, and more. There is a link to the "War on Terror: The Hunt for the Killers," which contains news stories, and an "America at War" interactive page with links to "9-11-01," "The Culprits," and "Striking Back."

NBC News
<http://www.nbc.com/nbc/NBC_News/>

This is the NBC News site found within the NBC.com site <http://www.nbc.com>. This page comes up when "NBC Nightly News" is selected from the NBC Show list. This page contains links to the Today Show, NBC Nightly News with Tom Brokaw, Dateline NBC, Meet the Press, MSNBC TV, CNBC, and Early Today. Selecting NBC Nightly News links to a site at <http://www.msnbc.com>. This page features "America at War: Latest News," also on the MSNBC site. This author would recommend connecting directly with the MSNBC site. Interestingly, the address <http://www.nbcnews.com> goes directly to <http://www.msnbc.com>.

MSNBC.com
<http://www.msnbc.com/default.asp>

This appears to be the home page for all of the NBC news shows and Web sites. From this page you can link to everything from the Nightly News, Dateline NBC, and MSNBC TV, to pages by topic, e.g., business, sports, health, and so on. There is a link to "Complete War Coverage," divided into "At Home" and "Abroad." The "At Home" page includes links to information about anthrax, the airlines, the events of 911, and coping with 911. The page about the events of 911 is, in a way, a memorial, containing stories, pictures, and interactive video. "America at War as seen on TV" contains current news stories. MSNBC video updates are available for current news.

Reuters.com
<http://www.reuters.com>

Reuters has been in the "business of information" for 150 years. They bill themselves as "the world's leading news and financial information organisation." "Top News" is listed on the home page, and there are pages for World News and U.S. Politics. A search by keyword for "September 11" pulls up more then 1500 news items in chronological order (most recent first).

United Press International
<http://www.upi.com>

The United Press International is a news service that provides "unbiased coverage of major breaking news" to the media. Only current news is on the main page, but the site is searchable by keyword. "September 11" brings up over 1200 results.

Index

Page numbers followed by f indicate figures.